Dorothy Livesay's Poetics of Desire

DOROTHY LIVESAY'S POETICS OF DESIRE

Nadine McInnis

Turnstone Press

Turnstone Press
607-100 Arthur Street
Winnipeg, Manitoba
Canada R3B 1H3

Cover photographs
of man and woman: Elaine Halpert

Cover photograph of Women's Army Corps:
Western Canada Pictorial Index

Design: Manuela Dias

This book was printed and bound in Canada by
Friesen Printers for Turnstone Press.

Canadian Cataloguing in Publication Data

McInnis, Nadine, 1957-

Dorothy Livesay's poetics of desire

Includes bibliographical references.
ISBN: 0-88810-181-4

1. Livesay, Dorothy, 1909- – Criticism and
interpretation. I. Title.

PS8523.I82Z76 1994 C811'.54 C94-920099-9
PR9199.3.L58Z76 1994

Acknowledgements

My thanks, first and foremost, to Dorothy Livesay. Her generosity with her time, ideas, conversation, and well-directed criticism is testimony to her commitment to "an ongoing universe." A number of people at the University of Ottawa offered me assistance. I wish to acknowledge the orientation given to me by Irene Makaryk, who pointed me in the direction of feminist criticism. I am especially grateful to Gerald Lynch for his thorough editorial guidance, his enthusiasm, and his ability to approach literature from both the critic's and writer's perspective. Thanks, as well, to Danny Lenoski, of St. Paul's College at the University of Manitoba, who helped me refine my interpretations at the final stage of this book's development.

I would also like to acknowledge the "invisible" support I received from Celia McInnis, in the form of mechanical assistance, and from Tim Fairbairn, for discussing poetry with me on a daily basis, for proof-reading, child-minding, and generally carrying his share in our domestic sphere.

Table of Contents

Introduction

Dorothy Livesay once identified the principle that underlies her life, calling it "serendipity." She believes in "small miracles. It's those epiphanies, small things that reveal a whole world that fascinate me."[1] Livesay's receptivity to epiphanies has allowed her to recreate herself poetically again and again during the sixty-some years of her writing life. She has been, in turn, the young post-Romantic lyricist that Dennis Cooley has described as "a bird singing to itself, perhaps to be overheard,"[2] the polemical fire-brand poet-activist, the meditative poet absorbed by metaphysical mysteries, the uninhibited champion of female sexual experience, and in old age, the wise and sometimes prophetic poet who turns her vision outwards beyond the boundaries of the strictly personal. Complementing her flexibility in content, she discovers and cultivates a new repertoire of poetic techniques for each phase of her writing life.

Yet the accidental nature of serendipity, her self-claimed escort through life, does not honour the fact that Livesay's poetic developments are not random accidents. She is not merely swept from place to place on the turbulent jet-streams of twentieth century politics and aesthetics. Her work builds chronologically towards a vision of how an individual's experience is shaped by social context. But even more importantly, she shows, through her tenacious desire to communicate and her willingness to take risks, how a woman writer discovers her own authentic voice.

The poems about love are particularly valuable as a guide to Livesay's growth as a poet. The theme of eroticism is first evident in Livesay's juvenilia and remains a central concern throughout her writing life. Some critics have focused on an apparent division between the political or public and the personal or confessional voices Livesay uses at different stages. The consequence has been that her love poems have usually been read as private and primarily lyrical expressions. But read as the fine line illuminating the circuitous logic of a creative life, the love poems are a map. They extend beyond the private relationship between man and woman to reveal the forces that determine the relationship between the individual woman artist and her male-dominated culture.

The earliest love poems in *Green Pitcher* (1928) and *Signpost* (1932), despite all their innocent charm, explore the conflicts that grow out of erotic attraction. Livesay cannot reconcile in these poems the desire to remain aloof, a part of the natural world, with the desire to love a man whom she perceives to be part of society. In a letter she wrote in 1978, she remembers that conflict vividly and connects it to her nascent vocation as poet: "Your dilemma, akin to mine as you say (if it is a dilemma) re wanting 'both distance and commitment' is like an echo of my diaries, aged 20. Over and over I longed to relate; over and over – had to be alone! This must be the familiar pattern of the creative woman. So: I continue to long for friends' nearness, to write them letters – but rarely to come close when we do meet. Intimacy only on the written page?"[3] For Livesay, as well as for many women writers, physical intimacy (or proximity) calls into service the traditional female roles that diminish the autonomy a writer requires in order to write.

Increasingly, with the poems written in the late 1940s and on, Livesay draws to the surface her struggles against the seductive sway of invisibility and silence that are embedded in the imagery of her earliest poems. She begins to explore the pleasures and problems of the erotic relationship in the context of male privilege and power. The love relationship no longer merely provides an emotional occasion for writing poetry. It becomes a proving ground for sexual/textual conflict. Livesay's treatment of love manifests all the challenges that face a woman artist who attempts to express a vision of reality not recognized by her culture.

In old age Livesay finally seems able to resolve the polarities of public and private focus that are so characteristic of her life's work. It is only appropriate that a poet of feeling, as she claims herself to be, succeeds in affirming her clearest sense of her own vocation through her developing and ever-changing treatment of love.

Notes

1. Dorothy Livesay, from a taped conversation with the author, June 28, 1990. This quotation was previously published in "Small Miracles: Memories of Dorothy Livesay, Past and Present," *Arc* 27 (Fall, 1991): 21.
2. Dennis Cooley, "Dorothy Livesay's Political Poetry," *The Vernacular Muse* (Winnipeg: Turnstone Press, 1987), 229.
3. Dorothy Livesay, from a letter to the author, December 17, 1978. Previously published in "Small Miracles," 24.

Chapter 1: The Critical History

"philosophies have never darkened me"

Every critical reading of Dorothy Livesay's poetry must address her struggles with her female experience and identity. Whether an article focuses on the theme of silence, or of nature, or of recurring images of the house, Livesay must ultimately be seen as expressing her central theme of "the relationship between freedom and responsibility"[1] through intimately female perceptions. Only the political/socialist poems written in the 1930s, if isolated from the rest of her writing, could be discussed independently, but few critics have yet been interested in doing this because Livesay's initially feminine and subsequently feminist vision remains the compelling force behind her poetic output. The handful of critical articles that focus on Livesay's love poetry provide clear examples of how valuable growing feminist consciousness has been within the realm of literary criticism. These studies concern themselves primarily with female sexual experience in relation to men and, by extension, male-dominated society. To date, most critical studies have approached Livesay's feminine/feminist content in one of two ways, and each approach can be classified by one of these qualifying adjectives.

One critical approach to Livesay's poetry concentrates on her "feminine" themes, images, and techniques. For example, Dennis Cooley's "House/Sun/Earth: Livesay's Changing Selves"[2] and Jean Gibbs's "Dorothy Livesay and the Transcendentalist Tradition"[3] suggest that nature contains male/female principles that must be accepted and embraced. In Cooley's and Gibbs's view, this involves inevitable gestures of submission on the part of the woman which are celebrated by Cooley and Gibbs as evidence of maturity. Gibbs writes that "fusion with the elements lies in sexual union. This letting go of self to be subjugated to man's will is often not easy, as it is not in the later poem 'The Taming' (*The Unquiet Bed*). But it is the only way to communicate with the larger order of things, to become one with the natural cycle. . . ."[4] Other articles, such as Susan Zimmerman's "Livesay's Houses"[5] and Peter Stevens' "Dorothy Livesay: The Love Poetry,"[6] acknowledge her political concern with women's position within society, yet their textual readings of the love poems imply that she is working out of an idiosyncratic vision created by her individual temperament, experiences, and needs.

The second group of articles, fewer in number, interprets Livesay's love poetry within the context of a feminist critique of society. As Toril Moi writes in her Preface to *Sexual/Textual Politics: Feminist Literary Theory*, "The principle objective of feminist criticism has always been political: it seeks to expose, not to perpetuate patriarchal practices."[7] Most of these articles are sensitive to Livesay's own committed struggles to understand how her experience reflects the problems of her society. Critics such as Debbie Foulks[8] and Wendy Keitner,[9] while aware of how they as critics and Livesay as a poet question assumptions about male/female roles within patriarchal culture, let textual illumination of Livesay be their central concern. A new approach, represented by Pamela Banting's article, "Dorothy

Livesay's Notations of Love and the ~~Stance~~ Dance of the Female Poet in Relation to Language," has appeared. Banting's approach, which she calls "binocular vision,"[10] discusses Livesay in the light of a theoretical question she brings to the texts. Instead of focusing on Livesay's work, she uses Livesay's writing as an example of "how the female writer begins to deal with the accumulations of patriarchal culture."[11]

Moi has pointed out in *Sexual/Textual Politics* that "value-free" scholarship is denounced by feminists "as always subservient to existing hierarchies and power structures."[12] Contrasting varying readings of the love poetry makes it easy to ferret out critical/theoretical assumptions. These assumptions are either invisibly "patriarchal" or quite visibly "feminist." A much richer reading of a poem, arrived at through all the subtle nuances and suggestions of its images, is possible if assumptions are clearly confronted.

The problems inherent in feminine/feminist approaches to Livesay's poetry are compounded by the fact that her writings have not been granted very much attention by critics. Although her books have been reviewed widely, critical articles illuminating over sixty years of her active writing life number close to twenty, including essays in *A Public and Private Voice,* the only collection of essays on Livesay's work. Only two book-length studies have appeared: Lee Thompson's *Dorothy Livesay* and most recently, Peter Stevens' *Dorothy Livesay: Patterns in a Poetic Life*. Both books sweep through her long writing life with a predominantly biographical-critical focus, the Stevens book being almost entirely biographical. Livesay attributes the lack of critical attention, compared to such male contemporaries as Earle Birney and Irving Layton, to her subject matter: "It may be that most male critics are somewhat at a loss to assess me as a poet because my femaleness, with its alien (to them) subject matter, interferes with their literary vision?"[13]

But, sometimes, the assumptions brought to the work are suggested by Livesay herself. Her insistence on her own intentions encourages a simplistic reading of her poems. In

"Song and Dance" she describes her own love poetry: "Behind it all a belief in love, in communication on all levels; and a sense of grace, a call to praise."[14] The simplicity of her style, the directness of her voice, and the uninhibited discussion of the autobiographical elements of her poems distract the reader from the subtle ambiguities that exist as a dark subtext beneath the celebratory surface. But to ignore the buoyant surface, given Livesay's aesthetic – her belief that "Laughter heals, the dance captures, the song echoes forth from tree-top to tree-top"[15] – would also be to rob her poems of richness. The balance between the two elements that generate the energy of her love poetry is best appreciated by close textual reading, and by letting the poems establish their own values, anxieties, and ecstasies.

Livesay's poetry is more an expression of her emotional, sensual life than of her intellect. She writes in "Song and Dance": "I suppose that all my life I have fought against obscurantism! For me, the true intellectual is a simple person who knows how to be close to nature and to ordinary people. I therefore tend to shy away from academic poets and academic critics. They miss the essence. The essential remains: Song and Dance."[16] Her unconscious is tapped through such non-verbal channels as rhythm and sensation, her immediate encounters with "reality," that give her poetry the contained pressure that turns coal into diamonds. A critical excavation is needed, drawing the seams of images to the surface, the veins of interconnected themes that, little by little, reveal a wealth of which even Livesay, for all her pronouncements, may not have been aware.

The more substantial works on Livesay which have appeared during the 1980s, such as Lee Thompson's critical book, *Dorothy Livesay* (1987)[17] and the collection of essays, *A Public and Private Voice* (1986),[18] discuss the theme of love in the context of an overview of her poetic output. This is appropriate, given the consistency of her concern with the juncture of the private and social worlds, but these overview studies cannot include the detailed examination of image patterns and their suggestions and associations which are necessary to reach a complex understanding of the love poetry.

Thompson's *Dorothy Livesay* is the first book-length study of Livesay which is sustained and structured by one critical mind. Probably because it is the first, it attempts to function as both biography and critical study. Such an approach demands that Thompson confront every shift in Livesay's poetry, and she does so, giving an admirable discussion of Livesay's homosexual love poetry, a theme which is notably absent in almost every other critical treatment of love. She is also more willing than most critics to balance the light and dark aspects of the love poetry. The only disadvantage of her book is its biographical emphasis. She explains changes in style and theme in relation to Livesay's personal experiences. For example, in her discussion of *Disasters of the Sun,* Thompson notes "a renewed sense of anxiety and urgency about conditions in the world"[19] and suggests that this "coincides with the decline and aftermath of her grand love affair, the start of a period in which her consciousness of aging, of transience, of decay and mortality began to come to the fore."[20] But Thompson doesn't trace the changes in Livesay's attitude towards love and towards men as lovers through the poems' tensions and images. The biographical impetus of a poem seems to be granted authority over the subtle interconnectedness that the poem shares with images and patterns in other poems.

The transitional poems between *The Unquiet Bed* and *Ice Age* grieve more than one lost love affair. Man, as he appears as lover in Livesay's poems, is changing as a symbolic partner to woman, whether that woman can be identified with Livesay or not. Another example of biography allowing simple explanations for thematic shifts is found in Thompson's introduction to Livesay's poems of old age. She attributes the renewed militancy in the poems to the appearance of grandchildren in Livesay's life.[21] This is no doubt a significant factor in the genesis of these poems, but Thompson's reading does not discuss in any detail why the militancy is associated with noticeable changes in technique and theme. An examination of how male sexuality is portrayed in the poems of old age, and how that portrayal differs from the poems written from youth through to middle-age, indicates that a transformation of vision has occurred. Livesay's attitude towards male sexuality, along with her own desire for men as lovers, changes entirely in her poems of old age, and is intrinsically linked to her political vision at this stage in her life. Despite its episodic nature, Thompson's book is nonetheless a landmark book, offering as it does a solid critical and biographical foundation. Another important but flawed critical approach, the more detailed analysis of Peter Stevens' article, "Dorothy Livesay: The Love Poetry," will show the disadvantages inherent even in the attitude of one of Livesay's best male critics.

Stevens states that the essential concern in Livesay's love poetry is "the question of individuality in relation to the male-female principle,"[22] and he introduces his discussion of *The Unquiet Bed* by emphasizing "her wholehearted concern about the position of women in society and therefore the integrity of woman in a love relationship."[23] Stevens' textual readings of many of the poems written in Livesay's midlife, however, give less emphasis to the social context he claims Livesay is acutely aware of. His interpretation of "The Taming" seems particularly subject to the cultural assumptions he carries into the world of the poem. His suggestion that "woman must give herself in order to release her own womanhood,"[24] that "the sexual experience makes her face her essential self, her womanhood with both its submissive qualities and its strength,"[25] and his final summation, "Love must give her freedom to remain herself even within the gestures of submission,"[26] express unrevised Freudian laws about "normal" female sexual development.[27] Such a reading does not honour the imagistic and thematic complexities of the poem. "The Taming" is the secretive stifled voice of the woman telling of the dark subtext of dominance which occasionally disguises itself as sex between man and woman. It is an integral poem in terms of the conflict between male and female utterance, the competition for voice and poetic rendering of experience. The command "Be woman,"[28] echoes four times in the brief span of the poem, silencing the narrator, teaching her the true "measure of the words." Stevens, like the other critics who fail to give much emphasis to the frightening and violent imagery that lurks beneath the surface of the celebratory images, does not recognize this other discourse at work between the male and female.

The way in which Stevens selects quotations from poems sometimes changes their tone and/or emphasis. He integrates lines from "Four Songs," for example, into his discussion by writing, "She finds her passion urgent and insistent, a 'hunger.' Her body is 'blunt' and needs 'the forked light- / ning of tongues.' Her passion is assuaged but 'thirst remains' for the gentleness and calm of love."[29] The section he discusses is actually written:

iii

And yet you knew
    my hunger
    the body blunt
    needing the knife
    the forked light-
    ning of tongues

    your blow
    eased me so
    I lay   quiet
    longer

But thirst remains
    thirst for cool
    cool water
    the gesture of your hands'
    white fountains

(*CP*, 293-94)

His omission of the images of the "knife" and the man's "blow" that makes the woman lie quiet changes the tone entirely. These are strong images that make even the most hardened reader queasy. But instead of asking the essential question – Why do these images appear in poems of ecstasy, passion, and celebration of sexual union? – Stevens sometimes edits, ignores, or diminishes the images.

Another example of an essential question never being raised is found in Stevens' discussion of "The Operation." He mentions that the narrator's view of the doctor corresponds to her view of her lover. "He [the doctor] is one who uses violence, a knife, to save her. She is a 'victim / grateful to be saved,' so she gives herself completely to him."[30] Stevens does not question exactly what she needs to be saved from or what has made her a victim. Likewise, he clearly and accurately observes that at this stage in Livesay's love poetry the love between the male and female lovers was "a sickness." "The disease racked them and at times their sexual union was an effort to effect a cure,"[31] Stevens observes, but he does not analyze through careful backtracking exactly why the love between them is finally recognized as an illness. Nor does he ask why the male lover is cast in the role of doctor/healer, a concept that appears frequently in the midlife love poems.

Stevens' concluding remarks reveal that he brings unspoken assumptions to the poems not only in a thematic sense, but also in his appreciation of poetic technique. "There is occasional over-emphasis and repetition,"[32] he writes, without questioning whether Livesay is making a deliberate attempt to create a desired effect by doing so.[33] She recreates the excitement of the body through her repetition, and begins to integrate fragments of speech, dialogue, and rumination into her poetry. The change in technique marks the beginning of her exploration of how a woman's aesthetic might differ from the aesthetic principles of the predominantly male literary tradition she had always longed to be a part of.

Stevens' contribution to the understanding of Livesay's poetry is most clearly shown in his discussion of her early poems. Although I would argue against his claim that in these early poems "the question of the roles played in society by man and woman is not raised,"[34] his textual interpretations are detailed and sensitive to the ambivalence the young poet feels about distance versus involvement. His discussion of her midlife love poetry starts from the basic premise that Livesay is placing emphasis on woman's place within society and the effect of such placing upon her experience of love, but he only implies that her individual fears and frustrations are linked to a larger social order which has been created and can be altered.

Perhaps Stevens' article is an example of how inconsistencies can arise when a male critic attempts a "feminist" critique. What Elaine Showalter calls "critical cross-dressing" is a problem that can lead to this kind of strange discordance between the basic premise of an interpretation and the close textual readings that edit and distort women's writing by failing to question masculine assumptions about female sexuality. In Showalter's argument against Terry Eagleton's reading of *Clarissa,* she describes Clarissa's rape as "the ultimate silencing, and a form of 'hermeneutic intimidation' for Clarissa's efforts to define her own nature."[35] Stevens fails to see a similar theme of "hermeneutic intimidation" between man and woman in Livesay's midlife love poems because he does not adequately question his culture's assumptions about human sexuality. As a result, the images of reading, writing, and speaking are minimalized and/or not recognized as being integral to Livesay's treatment of love. It must be acknowledged, however, that Stevens did not have *Disasters of the Sun* (1971) and the subsequent clarification offered by *Ice Age* (1975) and *Feeling the Worlds* (1984) to draw into his discussion. Livesay resists analyzing her own shifts in attitude by saying: "We're never the same person, you know. Every decade we become a different person. It's no sense saying, 'she said this at that stage.' Ask, 'what is she saying now?' "[36] Because of Livesay's obvious ability to revise her vision and technique according to her life experience, her complete body of writing assists in the interpretation of any one period of her writing.

At the opposite end of the critical spectrum from Stevens' piece, both in terms of style and content, is Pamela Banting's "Dorothy Livesay's Notations of Love and the ~~Stance~~ Dance of the Female Poet in Relation to Language." The most perceptive and useful conclusion she arrives at in direct reference to Livesay's love poetry is that through a return to technique which she identifies as "semiotic," a term borrowed from Julia Kristeva, "Livesay is able to find a relationship to language which is uniquely her own and which does not split her off from her sexual identity."[37] In Banting (via Kristeva), the word "semiotic" refers to that stage of psychological development "which precedes the imposition of the symbolic and the 'self' at the mirror stage through the acquisition of language. It is the primary organization of instinctual drives by rhythm, intonation and the primary processes. . . ."[38] Thus Banting interprets Livesay's childlike, chanting rhythms, rhyme patterns, and her flight into nature as manifestations of the return to the semiotic. By implication, one may add repetition of words, rhythms, and lines to this list of manifestations. Banting is identifying as essential and exciting the same techniques that Stevens judged as flaws. She is able to do so convincingly because she questions the relationship between bodily experience and aesthetic principles. Language itself changes according to the cues, memories, and experiences provided by the body, particularly the female body.

What is troubling about Banting's article, however, is her primary focus on feminist theory in relation to Livesay's poetry. As a result, she leaves unexamined some of Livesay's fundamental aesthetic principles that conflict with such a treatment of her work. Banting describes the relationship in Livesay's work between image, or symbol, and rhythm as a very important "tension."[39] The passage Banting quotes from the Foreword of *Collected Poems,* in fact, asserts Livesay's belief that a harmony is possible between rhythm and image, content and form. "Whatever the cause, always, I believe, I hear music behind the rhythm of the words. And always one or more of these symbols occur: the seasons, day and night; sun, wind and snow; the garden with its flowers and birds; the house, the door, the bed."[40] A firm belief in the possibility of the fusion, not tension, between these elements is the essence of "Song and Dance," Livesay's 1967 article which is now regarded as her artistic manifesto.

Banting's leap from Livesay's words to Kristeva's complicated, linguistically self-conscious treatment of how an individual moves from a pre-verbal, pre-Oedipal locus to a symbolic locus that alienates women in particular because it culminates in "a system of meaning operating through the adoption of the paternal metaphor"[41] is in direct opposition to Livesay's beliefs, as revealed not only in her critical writing, but also in her poetry. For Livesay, there exists the possibility of shared meaning. She strives for simplicity, moves away from ambiguity as she refines her poetic vision. She says: "I believe poetry is for people. . . . As Neruda said, . . . 'Poetry is like bread. It must be shared by everyone.' That is my whole philosophy, and that's why I'm a popular poet but not completely accepted by the Establishment."[42] She believes in fusion of the "semiotic" and "symbolic" elements of a poem, using a language that is familiar and common. Livesay may well be struggling to create "a new kind of language" which "could create a new kind of self,"[43] as Banting claims, but the language of daily usage is what she finally settles on as the vehicle for revolution. The diction, tone, exclusive language, and complicated logic of Banting's piece would be alien to Livesay's artistic sensibility and finally does little to illuminate the poetry.

This is not to say that one should not apply a challenging framework to an author's work. But if such a task is undertaken, the conflict between the principles underlying the primary sources, obvious through technical choices and thematic concerns throughout, and the basic theoretical values of the critic should be made clear. Otherwise, the theory dominates the text it is supposed to illuminate. Although Stevens' piece lacks the awareness of feminist theory that is intrinsic to Livesay's love poetry, his treatment of her poetry more successfully illuminates her aesthetic values, which are, in turn, intrinsically linked with her personal and political vision. And although Banting's "binocular" vision obscures the aesthetic values intrinsic to Livesay's writing, her theoretical discussion provides an interpretation of how the love poems work on a technical level. Finding the proper balance of all these elements is perhaps more difficult in a discussion of a poet of feeling, as Livesay claims herself to be. Criticism is, by nature, grounded first and foremost in the intellect. Appreciating the work in as authentic a manner as possible must involve balancing values according to the demands of the poem.

Less dramatic examples of theoretical superimposition are also helpful in identifying the risks one encounters in trying to achieve a balanced reading of Livesay's work. Sometimes, a reading which seems sensitive and sympathetic to the intentions of the work reveals on closer reading values which distort interpretation of images. On the other hand, a less aggressive feminist approach than Banting's does not necessarily ensure a higher degree of respect for the text. Perhaps theoretical frameworks are less dominant over the text when they are more obvious. One has no doubt about Banting's allegiances; they involve a highly specialized vocabulary and system of investigation. More difficult to identify are readings that use emotionally coloured words to describe subjective impressions of a poem. Dennis Cooley's essay, "House/Sun/Earth: Livesay's Changing Selves," and Debbie Foulks's "Livesay's Two Seasons of Love" reach dramatically different conclusions about the essential meaning of Livesay's love poetry. One reason for their conflicting interpretations is that they approach the poetry with different assumptions about the relationship between human sexuality and culture.

Cooley's essay doesn't appear to question the patriarchal cultural belief that male sexuality is naturally more powerful, vital, and assertive, and that it delivers great pleasure to both sexual partners. He reads the poems at face value, assured of their surface tone of excitement and anticipation.

He sees the development of Livesay's love poetry as residing in her gradual acceptance of male sexuality as a natural force which does not threaten her. Her pubescent reluctance, evident in the sheltering, cowering images of her early poetry, is, for Cooley, a product of her immaturity. He identifies the powers sweeping through Livesay's natural world as "overwhelmingly 'masculine'."[44] He sees these "raw male elements"[45] as something existing outside of Livesay, something she feels the force of and must come to terms with, and he gives no emphasis to the tendency in the early poetry for the *real* men to be identified with a social world, and not a natural world. These phallic images may not represent male sexuality, but, rather, be manifestations of heterosexual female desire.[46] Cooley is apparently unaware that it could be as convincingly argued in these early poems in which "Narcissus-like, she [the poet-persona] sees herself in the limpid mirror of her mind,"[47] that the power of sexuality, and all its correlatives in Livesay's natural images, resides in the woman who feels it rather in the object that inspires it.

Debbie Foulks's sensitivity to the cultural context within which men and women live and love leads her to emphasize the subtle, unconscious conflicts revealed through the imagery. She does acknowledge that the negative aspects of the poems are often balanced by celebration, but speaks of love as being more of an addiction with its two intertwined polarities of pleasure and dependency. She perceives Livesay's return to the images and themes of love in the 1960s as a "regression to her former image of a passive compliance in love."[48] Foulks's reluctance to give credence to the celebratory aspects of the midlife love poetry is most clearly revealed in her description: "These later love poems are preoccupied with physical description and convey a tone of pathetic eagerness."[49] Such words as "preoccupied," "regression," and "pathetic" are highly connotative and tend to degrade the persona instead of illuminating the subtle interconnections between images. Foulks is doing the reverse of what Cooley does in his essay. She superimposes her reading of the subtext of the poems onto their surface tone, whereas Cooley imposes his acceptance of the celebratory tone onto the troubling images of fear and pain.

The range of critical writing on Livesay's work already published in Canada reveals more than the misreadings and undervaluing that devolve from shifting theoretical approaches. Of greater concern, perhaps, is the range of quality apparent in the handful of articles published on her love poetry. Prem Varma, in her article "The Love Poetry of Dorothy Livesay," shares with Stevens and Cooley the tendency to downplay the negative intensity of some of the image patterns running through the mature love poetry. However, she becomes vague and confused whenever she encounters a poem that would require her to revise cultural views about sexuality, particularly female sexuality. For example, she describes "The Unquiet Bed" as "the protest of a woman who refuses to be subordinated simply because she has a submissive role in sex."[50] Nowhere in the poem is there any indication that the woman plays a submissive role in sex. In fact, Varma misquotes the poem in order to create that impression:

> longing that love
> might set me free
>
> ...
>
> move over love
> make room for me[51]

The lines appear in every published edition as follows:

> longing that love
> might set men free
> yet hold them fast
> in loyalty
>
> ...

move over love
make room for me

(*CP,* 292)

This is more than a mere typographical error; Varma bases her interpretation of the poem on her version.

Varma repeatedly fails to extend her analytical abilities towards an interpretation that integrates all of the poem's elements. The three sentences she feels are sufficient to discuss Livesay's "Other" misread the poem's crudest level of meaning, and then pass judgement on the poem as being "somewhat obscure."[52] Her summation of the poem, "Man's world is presented as circumscribed and narrow in their [sic] preference for an island,"[53] fails to understand that it's not "man's world" being described in the poem, but, rather, man's preference for woman's world to be "Convex and fossiled / forever winding inward" (*CP,* 220). Men do not prefer to live on "an island / with its beginning ended" (*CP,* 220): they prefer their women to do so.

One careless piece of criticism would not deserve so much attention in many other fields of literature. In the study of Canadian literature, however, the publication of such a weak reading of text is particularly unfortunate. Only a few articles presently exist that examine the theme of love in Livesay's poetry. Otherwise, her love poetry is examined in book reviews, which have obvious limitations of scope and depth, and more recently, discussion of the love poetry is contained within overview studies in theses and books. These larger studies attempt to establish a strong critical base that other more specifically focused studies can use as a touchstone. Some of the advantages and disadvantages inherent in these long overdue overview studies can be seen in Sandra Hutchison's Ph.D thesis, "Form and Vision in the Poetry of Dorothy Livesay, 1919-1984."

Hutchison's study places Livesay's development of a feminist vision at the heart of her poetic growth. By examining the techniques Livesay has employed over the years, the characteristic lyricism which evolves alongside experiments with narrative, dramatic, and post-modern modes of expression, Hutchison concludes that Livesay finds "a reconciliation of public and private selves in a feminist world-view which sees them as completely integral."[54] Hutchison's acceptance of Livesay's artistic credo, which the poet has stated in her essay "Song and Dance" and in numerous interviews, leads her to discuss the poems in light of Livesay's insistence that poetry is a celebration. As a result, although her analyses of the love poems are fully aware of the struggles that Livesay dramatizes through her metaphorical use of the masculine sun god who dominates the feminine principle, Hutchison feels confident in stating that "moments of real communication, healing, and transformation are achieved through the lovers' sexual union."[55] She places her emphasis on the equality of the lovers, claiming that the "bargain" set in the poem "Four Songs" involves "exchanged elements crucial to the growth of each one: his "*will*" in exchange for her "*fill / of passion*" and its subsequent overflow into poetry."[56]

The problem with such an interpretation is that it removes emphasis from the organic image patterns running throughout the love poems of 1967 to 1971. Although the tone of this poetry is often exhilarating and filled with a kind of breathless pleasure appropriate to the immediacy of sexual sensation, the images of drowning, injury, violence, illness, and silence suggest a much darker subtext than even Livesay may be consciously willing to admit. Hutchison's essentially affirmative interpretation of the erotic poetry prevents her from discovering another level of discourse at work in the poems. The struggle between man and woman for a voice, the competition between them as artists constructing the myth of their own experiences together in love, is played out bodily and textually. For example, the shift into a noticeably different poetic technique with *Ice Age* (1975) cannot be accounted for in Hutchinson's interpretation. It is not enough to say that with the loss of one particular life experience, namely, the love affair that generated the poetry from 1967-71, Livesay's inspiration and thus her poetic technique changes. The vantage point, awareness of audience, imagery, and emphasis on sexuality are so different in *Ice Age* that they represent a repudiation of her previous vision of love, which included the fear of being overwhelmed, not only physically and psychologically, but artistically as well.

Hutchison's overall interpretation of the vision Livesay finally achieves is thoughtful, detailed, and well-expressed. She recognizes that for Livesay "Art – and not least the art of poetry – is an island place of magic and transformation, but with bridges to the outside world."[57] By old age, Livesay has managed to free herself from the masculine sun god who formerly ruled over her and insisted "on a false distinction between a 'feminine' world of feeling within and a 'masculine' world of action outside the garden walls."[58] But Hutchison arrives at these conclusions without emphasizing the thematic, imagistic, and technical struggles at the heart of Livesay's heterosexual love poetry. Livesay's sixty-year output is a challenge for anyone to integrate into a unified, yet sufficiently detailed book-length study. She continued to change and react to all of the cultural, political, and personal influences to which she was subject. Hutchison's thesis provides an excellent analysis of the links between thematic and technical changes in Livesay's body of work, but it cannot, at the same time, follow the subtle inner logic of dreams and images in any other than a general way, and, for a poet like Livesay, these submerged currents can divert the course of the river.

Because of the centrality of female experience to Livesay's poetry, it is tempting to apply a feminist theoretical approach to her writing. Thematically and technically, her work echoes the development of feminist critical thinking. However, the complexities, and sometimes elitist assumptions, of theory conflict with Livesay's simple and essential belief that:

> The real poems are being written in outports
> on backwoods farms

that:

> The living speech is shouted out
> by men and women leaving railway lines

that:

> on midnight roads where hikers flag you down
> speech echoes from the canyon's wall
> resonant
> indubitable.
>
> (*CP*, 262)

Repeatedly, in her essays, letters and poems, she stresses that language has a shared meaning, and that poetry

> is communication
> not a game
> played with words:
> a poem is a message.[59]

Livesay does not hesitate to state that message's content:

> Our poem – everyone's –
> must be a message
> for survival
> Let it sound out clear
> signpost and banner
> plain talk:
>
> NO MORE WAR[60]

By emphasizing that the ultimate poem is shared by everyone, and by alluding to her own second book of poetry, *Signpost*, published when she was in her early twenties, Livesay implies that the message, NO MORE WAR, is the culmination of her lifetime of poetic struggles. "War," for Livesay, includes more than military conflicts; the word "war" suggests all interaction that is shaped by the desire to dominate rather than to cooperate. Presumably, everything she has written, including, of course, the love poetry, is part of that plain blunt message. The idea that a radically new strategy is needed to apprehend meaning in a poem because it is written by a woman, or by a man, within a patriarchal linguistic and literary tradition would contradict her most deeply held convictions about the role of poetry within the human community. Certainly, she shares with feminist critics an acute sense of how male dominance of domestic and institutional spheres has left the planet in its present precarious position, and she is interested in the relationship between textuality and sexuality which is central to contemporary (particularly French) feminist criticism.[61] Still, Livesay's passionate statements about aesthetics, and the consistency with which her avowed beliefs manifest themselves in her poetic craft, demand that a balance be respected between the poet's vision and the critic's theoretical framework.

Too frequently, the apparent simplicity of Livesay's poems has invited well-meaning critics to dominate the texts intellectually rather than to investigate the entrances the texts themselves provide. Although the love poems place emotional expression, sensation, and image above intellectual analysis, they are by no means simple. To achieve a complete reading of the psychic journey of a poet as she grapples through the various stages of her life with the personal and social implications of love, all the elements of the poems that dwell within and below the surface must be explored. It is preferable to approach the poems with both a respect for the individual perceptions of the persona and a knowledge of the social-political context that exerts pressures on her experiences, not to mention some sensibility to relevant contemporary theoretics. When love does appear in the poems of the 1930s, it is viewed by Livesay merely as a thread in the larger social fabric that is her central concern at this stage in her life. As the following chapter will show, however, close readings of her earliest poems, (1928-1932), reveal the thematic and imagistic links between love and language which will generate her life-long struggle to find her poetic vocation as a woman who must live and write within a society dominated by men.

Notes

1. Paul Denhem, "Dorothy Livesay," in *Canadian Writers and Their Work,* eds. Jack David, Robert Lecker and Ellen Quigley (Toronto: ECW Press, 1982), 98.
2. Dennis Cooley, "House/Sun/Earth: Livesay's Changing Selves," in *A Public and Private Voice: Essays on the Life and Work of Dorothy Livesay,* eds. Lindsay Dorney, Gerald Noonan, and Paul Tiessen (Waterloo, Ont.: University of Waterloo, 1986), 107-125.
3. Jean Gibbs, "Dorothy Livesay and the Transcendentalist Tradition," *Humanities Association Bulletin* 21 (Spring, 1980): 24-39.
4. Ibid., 31.
5. Susan Zimmerman, "Livesay's Houses," *Canadian Literature* 47 (Winter, 1971): 26-43.
6. Peter Stevens, "Dorothy Livesay: The Love Poetry," *Canadian Literature* 47 (Winter, 1974): 26-43.
7. Toril Moi, Preface, *Sexual/Textual Politics: Feminist Literary Theory* (New York: Metheun, 1985), xiv.
8. Debbie Foulks, "Livesay's Two Seasons of Love," *Canadian Literature* 74 (1977): 63-73.
9. Wendy Keitner, review of *The Phases of Love.* (I have categorized this review as an article because of the depth and the range with which it discusses Livesay's poetry.) *CV/11* 8:1 (1984): 50.
10. Pamela Banting, "Dorothy Livesay's Notations of Love and the ~~Stance~~ Dance of the Female Poet in Relation to Language," *CV/II* 8:3 (Sept, 1984): 14.
11. Ibid.
12. Moi, 51.
13. In Marsha Barber, "An Interview with Dorothy Livesay" *Room of One's Own* 5:1-2 (1979): 33,
14. Dorothy Livesay, "Song and Dance," *Canadian Literature* 41 (Summer, 1969): 47.
15. Ibid., 48.
16. Ibid., 45.
17. Lee Briscoe Thompson, *Dorothy Livesay* (Boston: Twayne publishers, 1987).
18. Lindsay Dorney, Gerald Noonan, and Paul Tiessen, eds., *A Public and Private Voice: Essays on the Life and Work of Dorothy*

Livesay (Waterloo, Ont.: University of Waterloo, 1986).
19. Thompson, 67.
20. Ibid.
21. Ibid.
22. Stevens, 27.
23. Ibid., 32-33.
24. Ibid., 34.
25. Ibid.
26. Ibid.
27. See Sigmund Freud, "The Taboo of Virginity," *Collected Papers, Vol. 4,* ed. James Strachey (New York: Basic Books, 1959), 218, for a description of the origins of "sexual thraldom" in the female. Also see Freud's, "Some Psychological Consequences of the Anatomical Distinction Between the Sexes," *Collected Papers, Vol. 5* (New York: Basic Books, 1959), 186-197, and "Female Sexuality," *Collected Papers, Vol. 5,* 252-272, for his explanation of how penis envy is resolved finally by the acceptance of femininity.
28. Dorothy Livesay, "The Taming," *Collected Poems: The Two Seasons* (Toronto: McGraw-Hill Ryerson, 1972), 296. All subsequent references to this collection will be identified in the text as *CP*.
29. Stevens, 37.
30. Ibid., 41.
31. Ibid., 42.
32. Ibid., 43.
33. Banting is particularly valuable in her interpretation of Livesay's poetic technique in terms of this question.
34. Stevens, 26.
35. Elaine Showalter, "Critical Cross-Dressing," *Men in Feminism,* eds. Alice Jardine and Paul Smith (New York: Metheun, 1987), 129.
36. Livesay, in the Barber interview, 19.
37. Banting, 17.
38. Ibid.
39. Ibid.
40. Dorothy Livesay, *CP,* Foreword, v.
41. Banting, 17.
42. Pamela Banting and Kristjana Gunnars, "Poetry is for People: An Interview with Dorothy Livesay," *Prairie Fire* 7:3 (Autumn, 1986): 12.

43. Banting, 17.
44. Cooley, 109.
45. Ibid., 110.
46. It is a basic tenet of psychoanalytic theory that the "love object" is chosen because of unconscious resonance. In the words of Freud: "The object is less closely attached to the instinct than was first supposed; it is easily exchanged for another one, and moreover, an instinct which had an external object can be turned around upon the subject's own self." "The Libido Theory," *Collected Papers, Vol. 5,* 132.
47. W.E. Collin, *The White Savannahs* (Toronto: Macmillan, 1936), 153.
48. Foulks, 71.
49. Ibid.
50. Prem Varma, "The Love Poetry of Dorothy Livesay," *Journal of Canadian Poetry* 3:1 (Winter, 1980): 24.
51. Ibid.
52. Ibid., 22.
53. Ibid.
54. Sandra Hutchison, *Form and Vision in the Poetry of Dorothy Livesay, 1919-1984,* Ph.D diss. (University of Toronto, 1986), 4.
55. Ibid., 233.
56. Ibid.
57. Ibid., 9.
58. Ibid., 8.
59. Dorothy Livesay, *Feeling the Worlds* (Fredericton: Goose Lane Editions, 1984), 59.
60. Ibid.
61. See Elissa Gelfand, "French Feminist Criticism" in *Encyclopedia of Contemporary Literary Theory: Approaches, Scholars, Terms,* ed. Irena R. Makaryk (Toronto: University of Toronto Press, 1993). See, especially, the description of Julia Kristeva, and Luce Irigaray's suggestion in *This Sex Which Is Not One* (1977) that "woman's language or 'womanspeak,' (is) a previously un-spoken and un-written discourse arising morphologically from the female body," and Helene Cixous, who affirms "a specific *écriture féminine* (woman's writing) grounded in female pleasure," 46-48.

Chapter 2: 1928 - 1964

"praise and lament"

In the Foreword to her *Collected Poems: The Two Seasons* (1972), Livesay emphasizes what she considers to be the major theme underlying all her work: "Especially do I note the dichotomy that exists here between town and country – that pull between community and private identity that is characteristic of being a woman."[1] Her earliest published poetry, in *Green Pitcher* (1928) and *Signpost* (1932), is imbued with her conflicting desire to "dig in [the] garden / Or follow the flight of the crows."[2] Intrinsic to this conflict are two other conflicts that are often implied rather than directly stated. The conflict that is central to the present study may be expressed as a question: Does one surrender oneself to love or is it preferable to resist emotional bonds to men in order to save "my self's integrity" (*CP,* 29)?

The creative conflict of the woman artist who desires to communicate within a literary tradition that does not fully recognize her experiences and perceptions is also an aspect of Livesay's love poetry and is an intrinsic part of her metaphors of language and silence. Peter Stevens argues that alongside the song and dance motifs that Livesay recognizes as innate to her poetry are recurring images of silence. He writes: "[I]n all her poetry we watch the process by which a poet assembles a world of poetry from a vast silence."[3] But for Livesay, the identification with nature that provides context for many of her images of silence is very much a part of her identity as a woman in relation to men, and by extension, her struggle with her identity as a woman writer is complicated by the personal and cultural influences she experienced which persisted in defining poetry/woman/nature as "Other."

Livesay pays homage to her parents for providing her with a rich literary education: "Talent must be nurtured, and my parents were gardeners."[4] The loam they offered her was a potent mixture of their own thwarted ambitions as writers and a long tradition of English literature in which women's voices were only beginning to emerge. Livesay's early poetry can be seen to continue the line of women's voices that emerged in the United States in the nineteenth century. Cheryl Walker has concluded that the most consistent and intense motif in these emergent voices is "vacillation regarding power,"[5] and Alicia Ostriker elaborates: "She [Walker] cites the pattern of the 'free bird' poem in which the poet sees some winged creature as an emblem of pride and courage and then proceeds to reject such a life as too lofty and lonely for her; the 'sanctuary' poem in which retirement means not rest and refreshment, as it does in poems by men, but a desperate retreat from pain and danger."[6] Livesay, however, does not retreat into the house, through the various doorways that her critic Susan Zimmerman so carefully documents,[7] without putting up quite a struggle. In "Defiance," she is the live bird being covered with pine needles: "Unless I am smothered – / Wings beaten – / I shall laugh still" (*CP*, 7). The coy tone suggests this poem arises from a physical tussle with a male suitor, but, as in so many of Livesay's erotic poems of middle age, the playful surface beguiles the violent imagery of suffocation.

The nineteenth-century woman poet who most influenced Livesay was Emily Dickinson.[8] Like Dickinson, Livesay discovers her unique poetic identity through careful observation of natural detail, through her ability to present conflicting views without backing herself into the necessity of making a choice, and through her celebration of the subversion of her female voice by skirting the edges of invisibility. Dickinson's wry assertion, "I'm Nobody! Who are you?"[9] is mirrored by Livesay's early stance of near invisibility. The young Livesay who writes these early poems is not yet confident enough to use the irony that is so characteristic of Dickinson, but the invisibility of the persona in her poems offers her a vantage point she will use again and again as a woman artist.

Personal influences in Livesay's upbringing may also be responsible for the sense in the early poems that the persona exists only as a secretive voice. As Thompson has noted, Livesay's father encouraged her to view prose as the superior form.[10] Livesay explains her early influences in this way: "My father wanted me to be a novelist because he was devoted to the Brontes and George Eliot, indeed to all works of women writers. . . . So when he found that I was really working at poetry . . . he swung around and let her (my mother) take over."[11] Each genre is associated with the influence of a different parent. Poetry occupies the realm of the mother, both literal and symbolic. Livesay, even at the age of fifteen, expresses the conflict between her impulse to write poetry and her aspiration to write prose: "I love prose – it seems akin to God. At times I long to spend my life making prose, – prose, – beautiful prose. But alas! There is music in my soul as well. Nothing will daunt my music; it swells and swells, sometimes leaving me glad – more often, leaving me sad. I wish the music would go away and let me have prose – and yet – I love my music!"[12] The reference to prose being "akin to God" firmly establishes a hierarchy of genres that not only places prose in the realm of God the Father, but delegates poetry and poetic techniques of rhythm and lyricism to an inferior and less desirable position.

Poetry itself, then, would be linked to the "Other," along with nature, woman, and non-verbal expression. Julia Kristeva describes the relationship between poetic craft and the "Other": "Poets have known from time immemorial that music is the language of love, and it has led them to suggest that the yearning captured by the loved beauty is nevertheless transcended – preceded and guided – by the ideal signifier: a sound on the fringe of my being, which transfers me to the place of the Other, astray, beyond meaning, out of sight."[13] Livesay resists the role that the male poet/lovers wish her to play. She tries to resist being "Other," but even in relation to something as basic as genre, her natural inclinations as a developing writer threaten her ability to express herself.

Instead of God, it is the Earth Goddess who has claimed the young poet, and her reluctance to give herself over entirely to her own poetic vocation heightens the images and themes of subversiveness, invisibility, and silence that she hears and articulates in her early poems. The ambivalence about love and communication through language that is so intensely expressed in Livesay's early poems is shared by other women poets of the nineteenth and early twentieth centuries, most notably, by two of Livesay's important influences, Dickinson and Isabella Valancy Crawford.[14] It is a sad irony that these talented poets did not enjoy an audience during their life-times, despite their fervent desire to communicate. No doubt the role that their gender played in the disappointments of their writing lives would not have been lost on young Livesay. It may also be that the shaping influence of both her parents, who invested much in their daughter's success as a writer,[15] served to heighten the ambivalence towards love and language obvious in the themes and images of Livesay's early poems.

In "The Unbeliever," first published in *Signpost* (1932), Livesay directly links the conflicts between community and independence, love and autonomy, male dominance in utterance and female rebellion through silence and absence. Although the title of the poem gives emphasis to the rebellious choice the persona has made, the poem itself does not reach a firm conclusion. Livesay begins, as she does in so many of her early poems, with a question:

> What have I done, in not believing
> Anything you said;
> What have I lost, from lightly taking
> Your gifts of wine and bread?
>
> (*CP,* 25)

The rhythm of prayer, combined with the suggestion of communion implicit in the wine and bread, suggests that what has been said is part of a larger, older story, and not some casual or personal promise. In each stanza, the persona balances gain with loss:

> Could I have thought there was something greater
> For my heart to gain
> By running away untouched, unshackled,
> Friends only with sun and rain?
>
> (*CP,* 25)

Her heart might gain by leaving false words behind, but the price she pays is isolation from the human community and identification with the natural world. The emptiness she feels cannot yet be filled by her own voice or the knowledge she will find by following her feelings to their authentic source:

> Quiet now in these lonely places
> I listen for your voice –
> Yet why? When in my heart lay knowledge,
> In my own mind, the choice.
>
> (*CP,* 25)

She is not yet ready to use her independent reason to interpret and choose a version of reality that she can believe in. She balances loss with gain and is left standing on tentative, lonely ground.

Even when Livesay's young persona celebrates her isolation in the natural world, she recognizes that she is not safe from invasion by the all-powerful male who defines her nature and role. She has to write secretly of how contented she is, at times, with her status within the natural world:

> How lovely now
> Are little things:
> Young maple leaves –
> A jet crow's wings.
>
> I have been lost
> These many springs:
> Now I can hear
> How silence sings.
>
> ("Secret," *CP,* 3)

The reference to other "springs" suggests that she had been distracted by her preoccupation with love from the authenticity of how silence sings. Now, she is free, alone, and contented, but her happiness must be kept a secret:

> Lest I be hurt
> I put this armour on:
> Faith in the trees,
> And in the living wind"
>
> ("Weapons," *CP,* 25)

This subversive faith must be hidden. Otherwise, the lover, who is also part of the male world that uses force to achieve dominance, can destroy the delicate balance of a female autonomy which co-exists with natural forces: "But O what shields, what swords / Can save me, if you too proclaim / My faith, you too invade my skies?" (*CP,* 25). The persona recognizes that although she is using metaphors of war and dominance, the faith she has is based not on might, but on gentle co-habitation which can only be defended by being kept secret.

Livesay's persona in the early poems walks "on feet made aerial" ("Autumn," *CP,* 2). She is a wraith who urges her lover to hold her before she vanishes and leaves behind "The aching sorrow of dead leaves / Frozen by the moon"

("Wraith," *CP,* 8). In "A Dream" she visualizes herself "pushing deeper and deeper into the sombre woods" (*CP,* 20) until she disappears, at which time the focus shifts to great flocks of heavy birds who "shook the forest with their mighty laughter" (*CP,* 20). She is the girl drifting near the river's edge who longs to call out to the farm-hand, " 'Stay! Stay! I am here.' / But the words would not come" ("Impuissance," *CP,* 6). He continues his routine, his contribution to the feeding of the community, without so much as glimpsing his secret admirer. She is the woman who cannot be seen dancing: "Only a fluttering breath of me / Flashed with the sunlight on the wall" ("Blindness," *CP,* 29).

The reason for her elusive self-expression is clear: "Your blindness saves my self's integrity" ("Blindness," *CP,* 29). A man has the capacity to invade her skies, distort her unique symbolic expression, as in "Perversity":

> That day I wore a red gown
> Because I could not hide
> The warning flame in me – But you
> Thought scarlet meant my pride.
>
> (*CP,* 30)

Desire in a woman is distorted to signify pride. Her subsequent attempts to communicate with the male lover through non-verbal symbols are similarly met with incomprehension until the persona gives up hope of sharing a symbolic system with the object of her desire:

> I dare not wear a white gown,
> My honesty to show:
> You'd take it for a shroud, no doubt –
> Uncomforting as snow.
>
> (*CP,* 30)

That the persona in the poem is pure, virginal, yet ready for union with him is beyond his capacity to understand. Desire, humility, and honesty are perceived as pride, bitterness, and frigidity.

The failure of communication on a nonverbal level is

made even more disappointing by the failure of communication through language, a theme to which Livesay returns repeatedly. "I nearly told you / All there was to tell," she writes in "Inarticulate."[16] But something prevents her: "Your look, a word –" and she grows accustomed "To reticence: I scarcely heed / What the wind flaunts" (*PL*, n.p.), sensing that her voice should be as insistent and natural as the wind's voice. "Somewhere my voice – / Articulate?" (*PL*, n.p.), she questions finally, without assurance that she will ever find her voice or sufficient confidence to use it. Her challenges to the male in metaphors of language take many forms. Titles of early poems include "Interrogation," "Confession," "Unwritten Letter," " 'Ask of the Winds'," "Explanation," "Secret," and "Analysis." Livesay's most popular figure of speech seems to be the rhetorical question, with whole poems being constructed from strings of questions that sound in her own mind, with her male audience chosen but not confronted.

The voice in the early poems is most confident when it is speaking out of silence, articulating what lessons silence has taught the receptive poet, who has retreated into the natural world partially as a defense against the loss of autonomy that a young woman feels when she must participate in a society dominated by men. Unfortunately, by stepping outside of the society which defines her in relation to men, she loses self-definition, and until she learns through experience what and who she is, she struggles with her own insubstantiality. The first poem in *Green Pitcher* (1928), "Such Silence," is the ultimate in feminine self-effacement:

> Give me such silence in a little wood
> Where grass and quiet sun
> Shall make no sound where I have run,
> Nor where my feet have stood.
>
> (*CP*, 2)

But by opening her receptivity to nature, she receives messages about her own hidden sexual nature.[17] For example, her aborted encounter with the farm-hand leaves her noticing how "The sun lay burnt yellow / Over the bristling ground" ("Impuissance," *CP,* 6). Although she concludes in "The Invincible" that the elms are "stronger and bolder" (*CP,* 6) than blinded men, the experience she has in the dark garden is implicitly sexual in nature:

> I hear strange rhythms
> Rising and falling:
> Deeper and deeper
> The elms delve their arms
> Into the helpless earth
> And suck the young wines
> Of spring.
>
> (*CP,* 7)

Even a stone, "Grey with water's passion" (*CP,* 8), vibrates with an almost animistic sexual energy:

> Stones lay in heaps
> In quivering, jagged piles,
> Grey with the kiss of wind
> And the sweep of water.
>
> ("The Forsaken," *CP,* 9)

The persona is "shaken, suddenly, / Discovering myself" (*CP,* 9). Discovering the sexual aspect of self, however, leads her to new conflicts. As much as she asserts the satisfaction she feels being alone in the natural world, the sexual static in her images indicates frustration. In "Reality" she awakens from the "hard, bright shell of my dream" to hear "The wind still crying in the naked trees, / Myself alone, within a narrow bed" (*CP,* 9). She reluctantly turns towards men as potential lovers, and explores her place in the social organization they dominate.

The man in many of Livesay's early poems is cast as intellectual, unspontaneous, concerned with etiquette, and rigid in his understanding of symbolic communication. As in "The Difference" he loves primarily through analysis and categorization, thus missing "A falling flame, a flower's brevity" (*CP,* 31). His thoughts "Are cold and waxen and remote" ("Sea-Flowers," *CP,* 48). The contrast between male and female is made even more pronounced by the poem "City Wife," in which a woman, who had no previous affinity with the land, marries a farmer, who presumably does. Her loneliness is mitigated, finally, by her discovery of excitement and beauty in nature during days "which [mean] to him / only the day between concession lines" (*CP,* 42). He is trapped in his role of harvesting, whereas she proclaims:

> I am not frightened of the earth,
> For I have flung myself
> Deep in a field of grass and dust
> And known myself:
>
> (*CP,* 45)

His concentration on his job, his ponderous ploughing, makes him less receptive to her presence. She feels the familiar pressure to be silent about her experiences and perceptions. She doubts that he could respond to her stories with interest, "Starting the fire of my joy, and the sweet unrest" (*CP,* 45) of sexual love. The poem ends in typical early Livesay fashion. She cannot decide to risk action, keeps silent as the "quiet elm, / Still and enduring" (*CP,* 45). The final image of the farmer's horses slowly climbing the hills towards home suggests that nothing has changed. The city wife will keep her ecstatic experiences with nature to herself.

The section of *The Two Seasons* called "The Garden of Love" contains previously unpublished love poems written in 1931 and 1932. For the first time, Livesay directly explores a woman's sexual experience in relation to a man without sublimating her desires into solitary communion with nature. In doing so, she presents the contradictory view of love that reaches its fullest expression in her middle-age erotic poetry. Sexual love is portrayed alternately as energizer and as a weakening fever: "I am merry; till like sickness love / enfeebles me" (*CP,* 67). Yet the immediate joy she feels in the lover's presence leads her to question her fear: "Feared you . . . Feared this? This shivering delight"

(*CP,* 63). Throughout the poem, there exists a dark counterpoint that is shrugged off in various ways until she reaches her final conclusion that for a woman love involves submission. The first counterpoint of dark imagery involves a predatory cat named Lucifer, the rain, the wind, and darkness, and is abandoned with the line, "Ah no: he's dead! Sun searches out my heart" (*CP,* 63). These images are developed further much later in *Disasters of the Sun* (1971), in which the male sexual force that reveals itself in dominance is seen in terms of a tyrannical sun god.

The persona experiences several shifts of confidence and doubt, recognizing that a crucial part of her sexual initiation involves succumbing to a silence which is not entirely mutual:

> I never knew much about silence
> Until I knew
> Your silence over mine,
> Your breath blowing mine out.
> Then the night flowed in
> And our one listening heart
> Pounded the question.
> ("The Garden of Love," *CP,* 65)

She is subsumed by the male lover. Livesay uses the same image of the penis as heartbeat in a later sexually explicit poem, and the similarities this early poem bears to her later poem "The Taming" are numerous. The man's sexual dominance is perceived (and in this case accepted) as linked to a dominance of utterance. Although the persona suggests the sexual act is a fusion of utterance, the preposition "over," the phrase "blowing mine out," and the verb "pounded" establish male dominance in the viewpoint of the sexual experience. The poem concludes with an explicit image of intercourse as injury: "The way to pierce myself, / To run cleanly on the sword" (*CP,* 70). And the persona masochistically criticizes herself for not having learned "This denial / That is affirmation," her definition of "Love / By itself" (*CP,* 70).

The persona in Livesay's poems receives a reprieve from her deteriorating sense of autonomy when the human world to which her sexual/emotional needs have turned her is propelled into a crisis of its own. The social upheaval of the Depression in the 1930s translated into life and death struggles for many Canadians, and Livesay turned her attention as a writer towards expressing her commitment to social change. Images of silence retreat from her work for almost two decades. For perhaps the first time, she is sure of her vocation and of the significance of her voice for her audience.

Most critics still do not recognize the social aspects of Livesay's exploration of women's role in relation to men in the poems that precede the obviously political poems of the 1930s. In an oft-repeated phrase that sums up most critics' views of *Green Pitcher* and *Signpost,* W.E. Collin writes: "Narcissus-like, she sees herself in the limpid mirror of her mind,"[18] and he praises her shift in attention during the 1930s: "She has developed beyond her egocentrism to devote herself to a human cause."[19] Livesay, herself, remembers the 1930s as a happy time *because* her relations with men did not result in loss of autonomy. The egocentrism that others note is actually an exploration of how precarious female autonomy can be in a male-dominated world. The loss of power that Livesay witnessed in most males during the 1930s helped her redefine oppression. Also, her political commitment gave her a context in which she struggled alongside men. Livesay explains: "For the first time in my life I was an equal with men. . . . So I became very close to men, as comrades, and that was a most happy time in my life, because men were never condescending. We all had jobs to do, we were allowed to speak up and give opinions and the whole movement was very restorative to my psyche."[20] Love, as it appears in the poetry written during the 1930s, is compensation for the grim realities of an unjust world, but it is no longer the primary arena in which struggles for equality are played out.

In the poem "In Green Solariums," even an exploitative sexual relationship between a maid and the employer's son is described in positive terms:

> O lovely whiteness of you! Lovely body
> Young and burning for me. What a joy
> To seize your mouth and know your hunger there –
> (*CP,* 72)

Despite her illegitimate pregnancy and her awareness that "my own life [is] bought and sold for them" (*CP,* 73), the persona manages to turn the monologue into a kind of victory speech for the birth of a new social movement. Her subsequent lover "will not let himself be lost for love. / There's bigger things than love to be worked out" (*CP,* 75). This view that love is only a small consolation for larger social struggles is the consistent view of most of the poetry written in the 1930s. The poem "Comrade" is the clearest example, and has been well explicated elsewhere.[21] In this poem, sexuality is revealed through images of opening flowers and fountains. The memory of love is sweet, "without an aftertaste" (*CP,* 93), but the important bond between the lovers is their shared struggle for social change.

The portrayal of love as a small part of the interconnected web of global, political, and social upheaval carries well into the 1940s. "Seven Poems for Duncan" is a panoramic view of human history, the most memorable section being "The child looks out . . ." (*CP,* 111), which foreshadows the frustrations and disappointments that will be expressed in some of Livesay's poems of maternity. The final section withdraws from the note of clear anguish sounded in the previous section with imprecise metaphors meant to evoke sexual contentment. The lovers, however, are not alert and active, as they usually are in 1930s' poems; they are "Like sleepers plunging deep / Into recurring waves of dream" (*CP,* 112). They "Cannot awake" and "are asleep on the long limb of time" (*CP,* 112). The consolation of love works as a kind of anaesthetic against pain. Gradually Livesay's poetic focus is becoming more personal, and in the process her identity as a woman becomes, once again, a central concern.

The undercurrent of powerlessness begins to creep back into Livesay's poems at about the same time as she begins to write about maternity. Livesay's poems about her transition into motherhood reveal the mixture of celebration and longing for lost autonomy that characterizes her poems about love. One aspect of motherhood which seems particularly problematic in the poems, regardless of the surface tone, is the isolation of the grown woman who is left solely responsible for the nurturance of young children. The complete absence of a shared parental role is evident in most of the poems on the theme of parenting. In both "The Mother" and "Invisible Sun" the persona fulfils the day's tasks and expectations from morning till night without adult companionship.

The persona sees the daily role of mothering, and all its attendant domestic tasks as, at its best, a private spiritual journey of the deepest universal significance:

> At the end of a day my hands hold heat;
> Dipped in the fire of love, they burn
> Like radiant isotopes, to illustrate
> Where hours went: . . .
>
> ("Invisible Sun," *CP,* 200)

Although the tasks the hands have completed are all domestic, Livesay enlarges the scope of the poem, connecting her hands to a benevolent invisible sun: "Oh, my hands have sung, have swung from the / sun's centre / To be the veins of warmth within a room" (*CP,* 200). More evident in the poems written in the 1940s and 1950s, however, are the contradictory emotions about the limitations that motherhood imposes on an adult woman. In "The Mother," the persona "cannot walk alone. Must set her pace / To the slow count of grasses, butterflies" (*CP,* 161). More significantly, "She cannot think alone. Words must be / Poised to the smaller scope" (*CP,* 161). She becomes estranged from her own thoughts, words, and patterns because she has "chosen here to stay" (*CP,* 161). Yet the most salient feature of these poems is not the demands of children, which are forgiven as natural, but the isolation of the mother. She opens and closes the day. Only after "books are closed and doors are locked / . . . From the parched day a fugitive / I bow, drink deep the well of silence formed" ("The Door," *CP,* 203) is she able to leap, run, "swiftly to meet myself" (*CP,* 203) by opening a shadow door which cannot exist in the household she manages daily.

Throughout these domestic poems run images of closed doors, darkness, weeping, estrangement from self. As well, the tree begins to appear as an important metaphor for self-exploration. The organic image of the tree, with its many branches, contrasts with the rigid compartmentalization apparent in so many of Livesay's domestic poems. At the same time, the tree is suggestive of her awareness of the position she has assumed as a mother. The persona takes her place in the family tree, yet finds herself caught between more than two generations:

> Confined to a narrow place
> This consciousness, the Word
> Is my predicament to be
> Separate, yet joined,
> Single, yet twain,
> Twined in the ancestry of roots
> Yet roving in the upper space.
> ("Variations on a Tree," *CP,* 195)

When she becomes a mother, the persona is confronted with more complex problems of identity than she has ever experienced before. Her position in the family is representative of her position within a culture that dominates her with its structures and stories. The "Word" is not the story she longs to tell; it is the law which confines her to the narrow place of the home. She has made her choice to cross over the threshold into "The day, the dark; housed in a quiet mind" ("Inheritance," *CP,* 160). She is held there not so much by the sexual link between man and woman that she originally feared, but by the children her erotic connection with a man has created. Her sole responsibility for the children in the poems is what thwarts her imaginative life and independence. From her children, she is "Separate, yet joined." They connect her to her ancestry, propel her to contemplate her own father's contradictory nature: "Two poles, stretched agony between" ("Inheritance," *CP*, 160), yet cannot fulfil her roving imaginative needs. Livesay attempts over and over to resolve her need for imaginative autonomy with her interconnectedness with others. The tree in "On Looking into Henry Moore" extends this conflict into almost mythic proportions, concentrating on the contradictions between the organic and the eternal. Only one solution seems possible: "The message of the tree is this: / Aloneness is the only bliss" (*CP*, 236). She aspires, however, to an aloneness which is all-inclusive:

> Rather, to extend the root
> Tombwards, be at home with death.
>
> But in the upper branches know
> A green eternity of fire and snow.
>
> (*CP*, 236)

Death and life, passivity and fire, "Female and male / I'll rise alone / Self-extending and self-known" (*CP*, 236). In Livesay's vision, man and woman are animated by different forces. The majority of her poems are attempts to balance the differences or weigh the different experiences of man and woman in relation to each other. Yet Livesay, at least in "On Looking into Henry Moore," seems to be offering the definitive solution to the conflict between a woman's desire to be connected to others and her need for imaginative autonomy. The conclusion of the poem proposes a fusion of man and woman: "Woman in man, and man in womb" (*CP*, 236). Despite the resolved tone, "On Looking into Henry Moore" does not mark a shift in Livesay's vision of the possibilities for female autonomy. Instead, the poem is an example of Livesay taking an image through all its rich associations, extending it as far as she can until she states unequivocally what that image can represent for her.

After writing with such confidence in the 1930s, certain that her contribution was socially necessary and potentially powerful, Livesay writes poems in the 1940s and 1950s that are full of doubt and disappointment about how and for whom she writes. Her poem "Tale" for Malcolm Lowry is about overcoming almost supernatural forces that try to bar her from entering the creative space once occupied by a well-established male writer. Gaining entry to his now uninhabited house where she eventually writes some poems is a hazardous confrontation with forces so strong she calls them "black magic." "It was not the lock that disturbed – for I had the key / But over the lock, that web of filigree" (*CP,* 197). What holds back the female writer is not the obvious mechanics of language or role. She already has the "key," the vocation and skill. The thing that bars her entry is treacherous and elusive, supernatural rather than natural:

> But I took the key, fitted it into lock
> And turned. The spider house split loose,
>
> ...
>
> And the house, surprised, grew meeker than a
>   mouse
>
> (*CP,* 197)

She has overcome the fear that would have sent others away, and found that once she asserts her will over the house, she gains entry. Once inside she writes some poems, but the victory of her gesture is not assured. The final words are a plea to the male writer to "*hear me, hold me true*" (*CP,* 197).

Livesay reveals artistic insecurity throughout the introspective poems that characterize her writing during her active maternal years. As in her early poetry, she primarily speaks to herself, trying to work out the conflicts that arise from the incompatibility between being a woman/wife/mother and an artist. Nature once again becomes the reservoir for many of her images, but the excitement that characterized many of her early poems is notably absent. The poem "The Three Emilys," more than being about three artistic women who defied convention in order to preserve their imaginative freedom, is about the two Livesay personas who made different choices. At the beginning of the poem, the three Emilys are much like the early Livesay persona. They are lonely, intimate with the natural world, free to wander the earth, yet crying out for human community. As the poem progresses, the persona realizes that they "cry to me / As in reproach" (*CP,* 202) for giving up the liberty to

> . . . catch
> The inner magic of a heath –
> A lake their palette, any tree
> Their brush could be.
>
> (*CP,* 202)

Instead, the persona is constrained or "framed" by motherhood:

> My arteries
> Flow the immemorial way
> Towards the child, the man;
> And only for brief span
> Am I an Emily on mountain snows
> And one of these.
>
> (*CP,* 202)

It is a characteristic of the dark vision of this middle period of Livesay's writing that she foregoes her rhetorical questions and her adherence to a balanced view to conclude:

> And so the whole that I possess
> Is still much less –
> They move triumphant through my head:
> I am the one
> Uncomforted.
>
> (*CP,* 202)

As in "Bartok and the Geranium," an apparent balance of contradictory views of life is tipped in favour of one point of view in the last few lines. Although "Bartok and the Geranium" seems like a reverse of "The Three Emilys" in that the vibrant, energetic artistic force is spent before the serene and enduring natural force that animates the geranium, Livesay's decision to end the poem with the dominance of one force over the other is part of the pessimism of many of the poems written during her years of active maternity.

The most dramatic example of Livesay's closing a poem of balance with a resounding slam is the poem "Other." This poem directly links men's definition of women to women's imaginative limitations. She begins with the blunt statement, "Men prefer an island / With its beginning ended" (*CP*, 220), and the rest of section 1 is an imagistic gloss on this one idea:

> Men prefer a road
> Circling, shell-like
> Convex and fossiled
> Forever winding inward.
>
> (*CP*, 220)

As Livesay goes on to write, men prefer women to be "limpid," "held," sheltered on an island, accessible, passive, and circumscribed. Section 2 is a passionate statement of the landscape the persona occupies according to her own perceptions. "But I am a mainland / O I range" (*CP*, 220), she says, and describes in vivid detail the variety of her experience in the most sensual of terms. She is not limpid or passive, but has wrapped the sage about her to sleep, explored, and climbed. She has furrowed prairie with her tongue, "Nourished it out of the mind's dark places" (*CP*, 221). The emphasis is on passionate experience and feeling. She does not need to be shown this landscape:

> . . . For I know
> The country I caress:
> A place where none shall trespass

> None possess:
> A mainland mastered
> From its inaccess.
>
> (*CP*, 221)

The persona refuses to accept man's definition of her, yet the poem ends on a bitter note. "Men prefer an island" (*CP*, 221), she repeats, recognizing that her determination to define her own nature can only be partially successful because men do hold the power to place a woman on an island and keep her there, at least physically.

The poems that Livesay wrote during the late 1940s and 1950s are full of the bitter resignation that is the result of feeling that only her private inner world offers freedom. The lover who has become a husband is repeatedly portrayed as rigid and erotically limited. In "The Husband," he is a "forbidden man" who cannot let others enjoy a garden from which he feels banned. Instead of celebrating the natural world, he imposes his rigid religious vision on the woman who experiences the world in very different, and more sensual, ways:

> Presbyterian, he paints the earth more black
> the heaven more radiant white
> than my plain eyes perceive.
>
> (*CP*, 203)

The persona states, "My landscape's technicolour" (*CP*, 203), and although she can describe it in detail, acknowledges that "My freedom lies within" (*CP*, 203). She decries the "arbitrary gates and perilous walls" (*CP*, 203) that bind her, yet cannot escape them. In "Letter at Midnight," she pleads with the lover/husband to

> Behave to me with love:
> I am one so self-encircled
> Only a thoroughbred could hurdle
> These tough hedges
>
> (*CP*, 204)

In "The Morning After" she lives a "Life on the fringe of feeling" (*CP,* 204), after crying all night. Her disappointment in her divided dreams is profound, yet she must hide it because "growing still goes on, persistence lives / In tug of a child's hand" (*CP,* 204). She proceeds to say that tears cannot build again the house she imagined she might enter through marriage, "Nor man the bastion" (*CP,* 204) she would have to construct to keep her happiness intact.

Images of sexual violation also emerge in these poems of disappointment. The sexual images that sometimes emerge in Livesay's descriptions of nature are intended as metaphors for other processes in human life, but their consistency reveals something about the links between sexual dominance, female submission, and the disappointment the persona feels in her attempts to compensate for unhappiness through her imaginative life. Personal growth and change are portrayed as painful sexual experiences in "Easter":

> Painful the probing spring
> pernicious for
> those who refuse
> growth, for fear.
>
> And is there fear
> in each incisive thrust
> of white shoot from the dark
> cold kingdom of the loam?
>
> (*CP,* 206)

In "Page One," memories of a prairie childhood are framed by a metaphor of sexual abuse of a child by the father. She describes the persona's first ten winters of childhood as being

> In bondage to this Lear
> This blue lipped, fondling father
> Whose hard chains
> Clanked on her feet
> Pinched the poor fingers stiff with pain.
>
> (*CP,* 158)

Significantly, the title indicates the beginning of a literary creative process that must follow the Cordelia-like persona's rejection of the stories of the father's house. She will not mimic his voice. Ice queens and glass slippers are given up in favour of the spontaneity of the calls of wild geese that draw her attention outwards, towards instinct and the seasons, away from the dominance of the cerebral paternity enslaved to historical time that characterized her childhood.

In "The Dark Runner," loss of optimism is expressed in the most explicit terms of sexual violation and domination by the male lover:

> Around the circle of this light,
> This self, I feel his nudging nerve,
> His prying finger seeking the concealed
> Small crack where my intent might swerve.
>
> He's sensitive to softness; hurries out
> The all-too-eager love . . .
>
> (*CP*, 218)

She tries to defend her integrity by constructing barriers: "The integer is I; integral while / I'm centred in sun's round" (*CP*, 218), but she is not strong enough to ward off the vision that threatens her. "But O, how swift the door is swung / And fumbling darkness found," she writes, as though the dark vision is something that invades her, body and soul.

In the section of the *Collected Poems* entitled "Poems from Exile," which contains poems written in the period 1958-1959, the persona begins to break through her powerlessness. Dramatic changes in Livesay's life are no doubt reflected in the movement outwards in the poems. Her husband, Duncan MacNair, died suddenly in 1959 and her children moved away to attend school, leaving her free to discover new directions in her life. The poems written during this period are filled with journeys. "Praise and Lament" best describes the ambivalence the persona feels towards her newly gained independence. Words and stories emerge from her formerly barricaded imagination with a violence she finds hard to integrate into her understanding:

> The wind at Land's End tore these words from me:
> (Listened to and heard by none):
> A cry against the dark? Or praise for light?
> Wild messages in code unknown.
>
> ("Praise and Lament," *CP,* 240)

The violence of her separation from her former domestic life with a man is best expressed by her poem "Widow," in which she sees herself from the outside: "This head from this body is severed" (*CP,* 241). Amidst poems about her voyage out and observations of new places are images of a vibrant creative force impelling its way into the light. "The Dismembered Poem" strongly foreshadows the vitality of the creative process that will be explored in *The Unquiet Bed:*

> Because in a moment of thaw
> the poem saw light
> was nailed on a cafe wall
> chanted at night
>
> It is now required to recant
> to recapture the words
> flown out into air
> faster than summer birds.
>
> (*CP,* 247)

The persona still feels ambivalent about her right to speak in her own authentic and spontaneous voice. She argues with herself about the power of poetry, finally allowing the poem to exist, whole:

> Recant! Recant! that cry
> is only a public noise:
> behind the door in the dark
> affirms the exultant voice.
>
> (*CP,* 247)

The attitude towards imagination has changed considerably from that expressed in the poems Livesay wrote while she was still living within a conventional domestic situation. The persona's imaginative life is still "behind the door in the dark," but it is "exultant," and the movement will be outwards, from dismemberment to wholeness, from secrecy to open declaration. These shifts seem to be possible only because the persona is no longer bound by others' definitions of her role. Thus, the poems of exile are full of new landscapes where one need never be secured. One can observe and pass through, reflecting on the past but never trapped in the present.

The poems that Livesay writes during her travels to Europe and Africa between 1960 to 1964 range widely in theme and setting. The title of the section of *The Collected Poems* that contains them, "To Speak with Tongues," reveals a new conscious preoccupation with the nature of artistic expression. Alongside poems about Africa are poems about cross-cultural approaches to art. Livesay begins to articulate her belief that meaning must be shared by all:

> Let's mix our alphabets
> juggle our syntaxes
> make angels into poppycocks
> and peacocks plain
>
> (*CP*, 252),

she writes in "Pictures at an Exhibition ('United Nations')." In "A Conversation" she celebrates the kinship of poets who "feed on each other's garden" (*CP*, 253), and criticizes an intellectual approach to poetry in "Houdini Eliot." Only a shadow is cast across the growing confidence and autonomy of the poetic voice by the re-emergence of erotic attraction to a man. Significantly, the wonder of the attraction is expressed through metaphors of language:

> We walk between words
> as if they were trees
> touching rough bark

exploring origins.
Linked, in this green shade
a tree's name shadows us
I share its history
with you
who came
a first man to this forest.
And you find roots
your look uncurls each leaf
till every word we speak
thrusts upwards from its mother dark
and sparks our eyes with light.
("The Second Language," *CP,* 258)

The intermingling of "words" and the tree (trees being loaded for Livesay with associations of imaginative freedom versus the family connection between man and woman) and the sexual suggestiveness of the imagery reveal a deeper exploration of Livesay's vision of how sexual love and creativity are generated from the same source. The note of reluctance and fear also voiced in the poem –

We turn away –
the wanting mouth
closed
the longing arms
clamped
(*CP,* 259)

– in combination with the vividly beautiful natural imagery will become predominant characteristics of the erotic poetry Livesay will write over the next decade. The longing for a way to reconcile bodily experience with verbal expression is central to "The Second Language," and will reach its full pitch of urgency as the persona in Livesay's poems surrenders her autonomy once again to love. Apparently, erotic attraction remains fraught with danger for the persona of Livesay's poems. She compares herself to the "dagga smoker," the "madman who escaped in terror":

I also also you
enter into league with these:
by you and me
(who do not dare to speak)
are such deeds done:
we suffer
and do not condone
we wait our turn.

(*CP*, 260)

Livesay's "turn" at love lies just ahead of her, and the danger to her artistic, physical, and emotional autonomy that she has always sensed will flower into her most intensely beautiful poems in *The Unquiet Bed, Plainsongs,* and *Disasters of the Sun.*

Notes

1. Dorothy Livesay, Foreword, *Collected Poems: The Two Seasons* (Toronto: McGraw-Hill Ryerson, 1972), v.
2. Dorothy Livesay, "Signpost," in *Collected Poems: The Two Seasons* (Toronto: McGraw-Hill Ryerson, 1972), 24. All subsequent references to this collection will be identified in the text as *CP*.
3. Peter Stevens, "Out of Silence and Across the Distance: The Poetry of Dorothy Livesay," *Queen's Quarterly* 78 (Winter, 1971): 580.
4. Dorothy Livesay, from a taped conversation with the author, June, 1990.
5. In Alicia Suskin Ostriker, *Stealing the Language: The Emergence of Women's Poetry in America* (Boston: Beacon Press, 1986), 34.
6. Ibid.
7. Susan Zimmerman, "Livesay's Houses," *Canadian Literature* 47 (Winter, 1971): 26-43.
8. Gina Watts, Livesay's closest friend during the years she was writing these early poems, says in an interview: "I am sure we were reading Emily Dickinson in School. . . . I can't really say why we liked, why I still like Emily Dickinson, and find her absolutely fascinating to read. It's just the small, the compact, the beautiful little structures . . . And yes, of course Emily D. influenced Dee. Everything you read influences you. But it is quite obvious, isn't it, that in spots Dee is pure Emily Dickinson." Quoted by Dorothy Livesay in *Journey with My Selves: A Memoir, 1909-1963* (Toronto: Douglas & McIntyre, 1991), 65.
9. Emily Dickinson, No. 288, *The Complete Poems of Emily Dickinson,* ed. Thomas H. Johnson (Toronto: Little, Brown and Company, Twenty-First Printing, 1960), 133.
10. Thompson, 16.
11. Pamela Banting and Kristjana Gunnars, "Poetry is for People: An Interview with Dorothy Livesay," *Prairie Fire* 7:3 (Autumn, 1986): 11.
12. Thompson quotes Livesay's diary, 16.
13. Julia Kristeva, "Freud and Love: Treatment and Its Discontents," *The Kristeva Reader,* ed. Toril Moi (New York: Columbia University Press, 1986): 253.
14. The only Canadian woman poet Livesay recognizes as being her precursor is Isabella Valancy Crawford. Livesay indicates how

impoverished a woman poet in Canada can feel through her speculations concerning Crawford's lack of a literary community. "I think she died of a broken heart, really, for not getting a reception," Livesay says in an interview with Joyce Marshall, "Dorothy Livesay: A Bluestocking Remembers," *Branching Out* 7:1 (1980): 19.

15. Dorothy Livesay, *Journey with My Selves,* 88. Livesay writes: "After all, were they not writers? Failed writers, perhaps, but here was someone in their charge who might not fail."

16. Dorothy Livesay, "Inarticulate," *The Phases of Love* (Toronto: The Coach House Press, 1983), n.p.

17. Livesay's description of what appeals to her in the work of Isabella Valancy Crawford reads like a description of her own early poetry: "[W]hat I was drawn to was the passion and fire of her imagery which was based on Native Indian myth and the mystery of the wilderness. She was able to rise above the conventions of language, as if curtains of that stage were flung aside and the backdrop pierced through to reveal an ideal world. . . . When the young poet entered into that world her true sexuality was free to breathe and be." Dorothy Livesay, "The Woman Writer and the Idea of Progress," *Canadian Forum* (November, 1982): 19.

18. Collin, 153.

19. Ibid., 159.

20. Marshall interview, 20.

21. For example, see Foulks, 67-68.

Chapter 3: 1965 - 1971

"the forked lightning of tongues"

Dorothy Livesay returned from Africa in 1963 to discover profound changes in the Canadian literary scene. The Black Mountain movement south of the border had begun to invigorate and influence west coast writers through the presence of Charles Olson and Robert Creeley, who were giving readings and seminars at UBC during the summer of 1963. Despite the revitalized poetic climate she returned to, Livesay's repatriation was made difficult by a lingering case of malaria and her own uncertainty about whether or not she would be able to establish herself as a writer within this new literary order. "[N]obody knew me or my work in that crowd and I thought I was done for as a writer,"[1] she has said of that first summer back in Canada. She was also faced with the difficult task of beginning to write poetry again after three years of teaching and living in a foreign country. Although she wrote extensively in letters and journals during her time in Africa, she had allowed her poetry to enter a period of dormancy.[2]

Luckily, what she had experienced in Africa, in both a political and personal sense, made her unusually receptive to the aesthetic principles of the Black Mountain movement. She had arrived independently at a moment in her writing life in which the body was reasserting itself as the basis of rhythm and old constraints of form and theme were thrown off in favour of poems which emphasized immediacy. In what was to become Zambia, she had rather abruptly found herself an independent woman once again in a country that was rapidly evolving from a tribal society to an industrial society. She had been caught up in the euphoria of a young country declaring its independence. But most importantly, as she writes in her essay "Song and Dance," "Africa set me dancing again!"[3] The sheer joy of movement she witnessed in her students was infectious, and the description of the qualities of this spontaneous, unsophisticated dance apply equally well to the kind of poetry she would write over the next decade: "Not a dance of touch, but one where the rhythm itself created an unseen wire holding two people together in the leap of movement."[4]

Charles Olson, in his essay "Projective Verse," describes poetic technique in similar terms: "And the line comes (I swear it) from the breath, from the breathing of the man who writes, at the moment that he writes."[5] Olson proceeds: "From the moment the projective purpose of the act of verse is recognized, the content does – it will – change."[6] It was partially this reassertion of the body in rhythm and the immediacy of the experience of reading a poem that led Livesay to explore female sexuality. She sensed, almost instinctively, that her evolving understanding of what a poem is could lead her no other place. So, unlike many of her critics, including Lee Thompson,[7] who attribute the explosion of love poetry in the mid-1960s to her affair with a younger man, I would also attribute her poetic exploration of sexual love to the aesthetic imperatives she felt at that moment in her poetic vocation.

To read Livesay's erotic poems biographically is to limit them to narrative or manifesto, and thereby to diminish the subtle subtexts within each poem. Livesay is her own worst critic in this regard, being willing to define the impetus of the poems in *The Unquiet Bed* in this way: "Behind it all [is] a belief in love, in communication on all levels; and a sense of grace, a call to praise."[8] She is a much more accurate spokesperson for her particular poetic aims when she is less self-conscious. In her Masters thesis, "Rhythm and Sound in Contemporary Canadian Poetry" (1966), she deftly reveals the aesthetic principles which are apparent in her own love poetry: "To the present generation the poem is not 'an understanding of an event'; it is the event itself. This concept leads to the view that the language in which the poem is clothed is also event."[9] Reading the love poems as works of art that strive to transfer the event into the psyche of the reader allows the reader to do his or her own analysis after the event has been experienced. Thus the poems are not "calls to praise," but renderings of events faithful to the various "formidable dark and radiant gods which possess and heal us,"[10] as Robin Skelton has described these forces, be they the sexual, sociological, or mythological forces that guide any experience.

Various astute critics have noted that Livesay has not merely adopted Black Mountain techniques, but has used them in original ways in order to explore the pleasures and disappointments of female sexuality. David Helwig, in his 1968 review of *The Unquiet Bed,* states that "the strengths of the book belong to Dorothy Livesay rather than to her new allegiance."[11] And Lee Thompson reports that Livesay herself does not ally herself with any one school. Even in reference to the more obvious early influences of the Imagists Amy Lowell and Hilda Doolittle, Livesay insists that "her debt is primarily to their example of freedom."[12] Although Livesay adheres closely to early Imagist doctrine by treating her subject directly, with no excess words, and through the rhythm of the musical phrase, she rebels against the most important poetic goal: that of complete objectivity. As William Pratt writes in his Introduction to his anthology, *The Imagist Poem:* "No true poem can be without human content; but in the Imagist poem, the human content is implied rather than stated."[13] What makes the poems in *The Unquiet Bed* so revolutionary is Livesay's refusal to express female sexual experience obliquely. Perhaps the urgency of her struggle as a woman writer and the sexual content of the poems with its specifically female perspective demanded Livesay search for her own ways of creating the immediacy that the poems depend on for their effect.

The directness and candour of the sexual content, however, distract many critics from the undercurrent of doubt and powerlessness that ultimately links the sexual experience with creative and political experiences, a link which is basic to understanding the evolution of vision Livesay achieves in old age. For example, Tom Marshall's definition of Livesay as "the original earth-mother of modern Canadian poetry"[14] and Desmond Pacey's enthused description of the writer of *The Unquiet Bed* as "This woman [who] refuses to lie down – at least to lie down for any but amatory purposes,"[15] suggest that subtext is largely being ignored.

Livesay opens *The Unquiet Bed* with a variety of poems, some which explore her personal origins, and others that assert the universality and immediacy of poetry which is part of "the living speech."[16] These two concerns are organically linked. By emphasizing the immediacy and interconnectedness of poetry and daily life, and by placing her immediate perceptions within poems that examine her development, Livesay begins to explore how a woman finds her authentic voice. She continues to write about artistic expression as though it arises from an anarchistic force pushing up through the orderliness of tradition. Most often, she celebrates this breaking into light as the tumultuous energy that is the rightful fuel for what she calls "a conflagration" ("The Incendiary," *CP,* 263) of Canadian poetry. Images of order and rule being irresistibly overwhelmed by immediacy and spontaneity recur in the poems of *The Unquiet Bed.* In "Spring," the old teacher who once

held them [the students] with the chalk
    in her stiff hand
and wound them with her wand
into a maze of symbol
    drift of sound

(*CP*, 274)

loses all her authority as spring arrives and "colour invades the perpendicular" (*CP*, 275). The child in "Isolate" who wins playmates by constructing elaborate games is abruptly abandoned when a fire-wagon spontaneously bursts from behind closed gates across the street: "Games fall apart / as children fly like sparks / with whoops and shouts into the charging street" (*CP*, 275). Event takes precedence over intent.

Yet the poems reveal a darker side to the jubilation of fully participating in the processes of art and living. Always present is the threat of isolation and silence. Celebrating the disruption of predictable ways of seeing and experiencing reality can mean that one will be dismissed by the world that operates within existing structures. "*How can you stop looking?*" (*CP*, 276) the child cries out to the circumscribed adult world in "Perceptions." In "Roots," Malcolm Lowry ineffectually rails against the indifference of the world, and "poet pounds on poet's door / and there's no answer" ("Roots," *CP*, 268). Abe Klein's silence as a poet is described in terms of violence towards the unborn; in the golden hive of his head, bees "fumble for honey amidst empty cells / where the slain poems / wingless, tremble" ("For Abe Klein: Poet," *CP*, 278). This interruption in the genesis of poems is seen as highly unnatural, yet Livesay seems acutely aware of the fear inherent in the creative process. In "Making the Poem," which is about the process of writing serial poems, that fear is particularly intense. Poems arise actively from the passive experience of dreaming; like dreams they arrive in the middle of the night unbidden, sometimes threatening. But unlike dreams, they require a sensitive and fluid participation on the part of the writer so that they will reveal a

progression
not a repetition
a movement
breaking through
outwards
(*CP*, 281)

"Ballad of Me" is placed at the beginning of *The Unquiet Bed* as an introduction to the persona who will reveal herself so intimately in the love poems later in the volume. It is a serial poem which is quite carefully controlled beneath its seemingly random structure. Many of the conflicts that reveal themselves in the love poems are present in this overview of how a woman's inner life is distorted by the pressures of a male-dominated society. Each of the four sections focuses on a different stage of the persona's life: the girl, the young woman, the wife, and the aging woman, with the final stage involving a shift from past to present tense in the attempt to return to origins to understand all that has come before. The four events featured in the poem: failure at sports, an abortion, an unhappy wife seeking psychiatric help, and a woman returning to her childhood home, seem independent of each other, encapsulated, with little apparent resonance of image and tone. The thread that holds the poem together, however, is the implied theme of disorientation. In each of the first three sections the persona's version of reality is altered by a powerful male who tells her that what she perceives and experiences is inadequate and wrong.

Section i is an apparently light-hearted description of physical ineptitude. The poem evokes through jostling rhythm and energetic diction the immediate, visceral experience of movement. The dance that has become so important to Livesay, however, is off-kilter, clumsy. She calls herself "misbegotten," as though the personal defect is inborn. But the physical challenges she fails to meet are culturally masculine, falling within the realm of sports. The father teaches the rules, and he is the source of ultimate judgement:

> *Butterfingers*
> father called it
> throwing the ball
> which catch as catch can
> I couldn't.
>
> (*CP*, 265)

She perceives the tennis net in two places at once, and cannot catch because she cannot see the physics and rules of the game, even though the game seems so universal that she describes her place in it in mock-cosmic terms:

> the world, chuckling sideways
> tossed me off
> left me wildly
> treading air
> to catch up.
>
> (*CP*, 265)

But the comic tone and playful material change abruptly in section ii. The narrator's numb voice states that the reaction to abortion that is prescribed by her society is inaccurate to her experience. At first, she feels nothing, and the male participants in the abortion are portrayed as being untouched by the loss. The abortionist merely adds "one more line / to his flat perspective" (*CP*, 266). The father can "make another" some time, as his loss is only abstract. He does not experience abortion with his body, as a woman does.[17] This experience, instead of being expressed through guilt, which is a product of abstract morality, results in a more authentic expression of grief through poetry:

> I held the moon in my belly
> nine months' duration
> then she burst forth
> an outcry of poems.

The perspective and source material for this poetry is generated directly from a woman's body and runs parallel to her procreative capacities.[18] The lost child, which is portrayed as female, develops through a phantom pregnancy governed by the moon, and her birth cry is the cry of grief rendered in poems which throw aside patriarchal versions of how a woman experiences her own reality.

The doctor as the keeper of patriarchal power and authority over a woman's body and emotional life is an idea that is most potently expressed in Livesay's later serial poem, "The Operation," but in section iii of "Ballad of Me," Livesay clearly links the doctor, the husband, and the patriarchal order. The psychiatrist's prime function in the poem is not to heal the woman, but to ensure that she conforms to her prescribed role. He undermines her perceptions of her own unhappy position by asking her about her fantasies. Although she cannot free herself from her subordinate position, she will not accept the male stories about female reality. The life she lives daily is a fantasy constructed by men, and what she harbours in her imagination are not fantasies, but wishes. He will not allow her to express those wishes, however, and sends her back to her household duties.

The aging woman who returns to her childhood home in section iv is alone, cut loose from her association with men. Only the dyed hair is the reminder of how she attempts to alter herself to please standards of youth and beauty imposed on women. Her self-description is realistic rather than unflattering:

> I go incognito
> in sandals, slacks
> old sweater
> and my dyed hair
>
> (*CP*, 267)

But she still carries with her the threatening and hidden inner life that pushes outwards, demanding acknowledgement:

> I go disarrayed
> my fantasies
> twist in my arms
> ruffle my hair

The persona carries unruly fantasies in her arms like a ghastly baby, that same lost baby that allowed her to recognize that her most authentic perceptions would be defined as defective by the patriarchal order. These "fantasies" are her stories that haven't metamorphosed from dream to myth. Still, they cannot be submerged completely. She returns to her childhood home only to discover that "No one remembers Dorothy / was ever here." She has become, once again, the invisible and insubstantial female presence that inhabited the early poems. Yet as an aging woman, instead of being ethereal, she travels incognito as a kind of dishevelled scarecrow who proceeds warily, "fearing to scare / the crow" (*CP*, 267). Once again, she must choose between discovering the freedom of flight and seeking her place in the human world, both past and present.

The men in "Ballad of Me" are easily identified as threatening to the female persona in her attempts to discover authentic orientation through her own perceptions of reality. It is more difficult to recognize the same struggles in the love poems of *The Unquiet Bed,* because, in many of these poems, the persona indicates through tone and direct statement that she whole-heartedly desires her erotic union with the man. Only in *Plainsongs* and *Disasters of the Sun* does the surface tone consistently darken. In these subsequent volumes the elation subsides into disappointment. The persona in *The Unquiet Bed,* however, is poetically inspired by her bodily experience at the same time as she struggles against being silenced. "Four Songs" establishes the terms of the love relationship from its outset. The male lover enters the "bargain" through design:

> *Give me the will,* you said
> *and in return*
> *take from my fill*
> *of passion*
>
> (*CP*, 293)

He wants her to function as a muse, and loves the fire she generates rather than the woman herself. He offers her his sexual attention as compensation, even though the pleasure it provides is laced with violence:

the body blunt
needing the knife
the forked light-
ning of tongues

your blow
eased me so
I lay   quiet
longer

(*CP*, 293)

Livesay intertwines poetic and sexual expression throughout these love poems. The persona's sexual desires are expressed in metaphors of language. The tongues are literal and linguistical but, ironically, the "blow" of sex serves to silence her. The woman, however, cannot be dominated entirely. Always, she attempts to balance light with dark, hunger and thirst, creation and destruction. Livesay immediately softens the violent image of annihilation by allowing her hunger to resolve into thirst for the man's communication. Her resumption of speech is not a product of the "fiery stuff / burning the mouth," but of "the liquid flow / of words" that follows sexual love. From this source she tastes a "song in the mouth" (*CP*, 294).

One of the recurring themes of *The Unquiet Bed*, and of the love affair portrayed therein, is the search for aesthetic authenticity. This search often takes the form of a competition between man and woman, poet and poet, struggling for inspiration. The persona in *The Phases of Love*, even amidst her jubilation in love, complains:

words, your words
        appear on the magic slate
my body rubs them out
        and I try again
                to defend the right hand
                                side
of the paper
        to leave myself room for breathing[19]

In many poems, the male lover attempts to turn her into a muse while she attempts to discover her authentic voice by exploring her experience of love. Her insistence upon the visceral realities of love are contrary to her role as muse. She cannot inspire him with unearthly beauty, cannot serenely accept the role of subject and inspiration for his poetic utterance, as long as she is a flesh and blood woman struggling to express her own vision.

Livesay's use of graphic details in the love poems emphasizes the visceral presence of the female persona. Such details prevent the love poems from falling into place as part of a long tradition of love poems in which women are often projections of male fantasies, fears, and internal struggles. In Livesay's poems, the penis "rests in the opening / throbs" ("The Touching," (*CP,* 297); the female body bleeds and ages:

> Crow's feet your finger follows
> circling my eyes
> and on the forehead's field
> a skeleton of leaves
> ("The Notations of Love," *CP,* 302)

As Alicia Ostriker has written: "[O]ne subject that all women have in common to tell the truth about is anatomy; not, perhaps, as destiny but as priority, especially since in a world where perhaps not much is to be trusted, 'the body does not lie.' "[20] Through sexual love, Livesay writes:

> The margins between us
> blurred
> and the page we wrote
> together
> left nothing out
>
> (*PL*, n.p.)

Writing that generates from the body is indelible. Even a throwaway detail like stained sheets gains significance in this uncharted poetic territory:

> The record of all our nights
> is on these sheets:
> though washed, held up in sunlight
> the mark remain
>
> ...
>
> no bleach can take from linen
> what the body wrote
>
> (*PL*, n.p.)

Livesay discovers an urgent and exciting poetic voice through her exploration of the female experience of sexual love, but always, she is threatened by silence.

Livesay is well aware, as so many French feminists like Kristeva and Cixous have pointed out, that the male, in both love and literature, has on his side the weight of mythology, tradition, and authority. In "Poet and Critic," Livesay juxtaposes two different ways of writing and reading that could be roughly classified as feminine and masculine. The first is sensual, a product of the inner life. Words

> . . . caress the jar
> colour its round belly
> curl fingers round
> its throat:
> before the jar is tipped
> words have us drinking from it.
>
> (*CP*, 305)

The reader/critic of the title and the writer become one and the same in Livesay's claim that "what I seal / on the poem's mouth / is my tongue's pressure." The link between the body and poetic expression gives poetry an immediacy that is lacking in poems which sit upon her shelf like "small gods" which say "only as much as form and shape / can shout." "Poet and Critic," which is dedicated to Raymond Souster, is an argument against the hierarchical values of a male literary tradition that places writer above reader, virtuosity of poetic technique above sensual persuasion.

Regardless of how sure Livesay seems to be about the imperatives of her own developing aesthetic, she repeatedly expresses fear that she will not have enough room to express herself. The greatest threat is a culture dominated by inaccurate perceptions of female reality. "The Unquiet Bed," with its orderly patterns and non-threatening simplicity, concludes with a playful demand for space to express her version of her own reality:

> the woman I am
> is not what you see
> move over love
> make room for me
>
> (*CP*, 292)

"Love" must move over to let her be; both "love," the pet name for the man she shares her bed with, as well as the whole idea of "love," complete with its conventions and traditions which define women in male terms.

The myths and stories of her culture which try to define her enter into the most intimate aspects of her life and, at their worst, encourage a kind of passivity which is death to the artist. In "The Dream," her subconscious encounter with a unicorn results in a complete dissolution of her being. All the cultural resonances of unicorn mythology, most significantly the figure of the virgin who can tame the creature, suggest that the threat this mythology poses to the persona is that it alienates her from her sexual experience, her sensual body, which is the source of her poetry. The unicorn, which calmly walks at her side, generates destruction from his "cool nostril":

> such wind blew
> as tore the hair out of my head
> my eyes from seeing and
> my breath from speech.
>
> (*CP*, 294)

This is the unicorn myth from the point of view of the woman as artist, for conforming to the cultural ideal of "virgin" robs a woman of her corporeal reality, and thus her voice. She dissolves entirely into the ground but for two girlish sexual appendages. The persona tells us that "only my small white breasts arose / ponderous and round." The romantic diction and formal, old-fashioned syntax lull the reader into believing that the poem conforms to a traditional view of love. In "A Book of Charms" the same effect is created by the romantic imagery. The lover sends his female lover off to bed clutching a rose which sheds a soft light by which she dreams that he later "reads" her between "the leaves / love's book" (*CP,* 296). He demands that she exist within the book of charms that *he* can read in a rosy light. This is his text, his desire, his story which determines her passive role.

The female persona cannot conform to his idealizations, however, because she does exist as a physical body:

> My tongue
>   was too long
> my kiss
>   too short
> Inadequate I shrank
>   from perfection
>
> (*CP,* 300)

she writes in "And Give Us Our Trespasses." Not only her speech is stifled, but also her awareness of herself as a physical being is dominated by his:

> Whenever I spoke
>   out of turn, was it?
> you'd press your fingers
>   against my mouth:
>   *Listen.*
> I heard only your heartbeat
>
> (*CP,* 300)

The silencing of the woman during sex is linked to the man's dominance of the sexual experience with his fantasies and demands. "Yet charged / your beauty charged me," (*CP,* 301) Livesay writes, expressing beautifully with this triple pun the depth of woman's ambivalence in love. He rushes her, he costs her dearly, yet the force of his sexuality is as powerful as an electric current, and, mysteriously, "the receptor trembles."

In "The Taming," the persona is told outright, "Be woman." She only comes to understand what this means through the hard lessons of living. "Do what I say, woman: / just that / and nothing more" (*CP*, 296), a man orders when she does not prepare food to his liking. He commands the same when he demands sexual access to her body. She is denied sleep and dreams by the man who, at the moment of orgasm, commands her:

> Do as I say, I heard you faintly
> over me fainting:
> be woman.

The poem clearly links the domestic service to the sexual service. Both demand a woman's silence and submissiveness.

The ambivalence the persona expresses about the love relationship is often couched in images of corporeal injury, illness, or disintegration. Even though the persona in "The Notations of Love" describes the flesh being stripped from her bones by love as a gentle process, the submerged tone of bitterness is suggested by her repetition of the phrase "you left me nothing" (*CP*, 302). He undresses her so thoroughly that she melts down "into the earthy green." She becomes a corpse with grass growing between her thighs. A flower germinating from her decomposition is all that remains of her capacity to speak:

> and when a flower shot
> out of my unclenched teeth
> you left me nothing but
> a tongue to say it with.
>
> (*CP*, 302)

A note of desperation creeps into the poems as the persona suggests that only the male lover, through his sexual attention, can return her lost bodily autonomy.

My legs stretched two ways   disparate
until you came
and joined them
(lying down between)

(*CP*, 303)

she says, even while recognizing that her loss of autonomy was directly linked to his answered needs. "*I was naked / and you clothed / me,*" he tells her as his only words of praise. Love, ironically, has provided him with protection from his own naked vulnerability. In contrast, sexual intimacy has not only undressed the persona; it has practically deconstructed her. In his self-involvement, he doesn't notice. He emphasizes solely what she has provided for him, and he is able to ignore her anxieties.

While *The Unquiet Bed* contained many moments of exhilarition, the underlying tone in most of the love poems in *Plainsongs* is desperation. The male lover accumulates power in direct proportion to the persona's loss of power, which is expressed often in images of bodily injury and illness. At times, such as in "At Dawn," "The Woman," and "Sorcery," the persona is able to transform her anxieties into acute sexual desire. The sharp clarity of her imagery contains an urgency that overshadows the slow smouldering of powerlessness that precedes it. The culmination of "At Dawn"–

and over all
my body's fingertips
day breaks
a thousand crystals

(*CP*, 316)

– is so vivid readers might forget that the persona has been held in bed, unable to move, listening to "the ferment / of your dreams / churning my pillow." The wish-fulfilment dream the persona imagines at the end of "The Cave," "*O love, we hold, we have*" (*CP*, 317), the words she so desperately craves, serves to lessen the impact of her lover's selfish insistence on sexual gratification. His sinister control of her, which she only begins to admit, is momentarily compensated for by her attempt at self-consolation. The persona in "Sorcery" describes her body as hideous:

> My breasts are withered gourds
> my skin all over   stiffens
> shrinks – the pubic hair
> bristles to an itch
>
> (*CP,* 318)

She then explains that the metamorphosis of her body to this ghastly condition is a direct result of not being touched by her lover, and begs him to "magic me / out of insanity" by dancing, tossing, and catching her. Only he has the power to give her back her body, her humanity, "from scarecrow to girl again."

The unconscious life she portrays through her dream poems indicates similar anxieties. Her eyes are pecked out in "Dream," and in "Auguries" she is a small powerless girl turning in the heel of the lover's hand, "a shell in your hand / to be broken" (*CP,* 319). She questions whether there can be a morning station further ahead, some relief from these dark, turbulent dreams. The threat the lover poses intensifies in power and association. He threatens her physical autonomy, her sanity, her artistic utterance. She compares her persistent love for him to malaria, which "leaps in an adder's fashion" (*PL,* n.p.). It strikes and strangles her, robbing her of meaningful language. As she journeys towards him in "The Journey East," he takes on an almost daemonic power, possessing her from within. "I feel you within me / steering," she writes. She cannot find him, even though he inhabits everything she sees, permeates everything she eats:

> when I chewed clam chowder
>   I was nibbling your fingers
> when I swallowed baked lobster whole
> it was your forked tongue stabbing
>
> (*CP,* 325)

Love threatens her on every level, and trying to remove it from her life leaves her with dangerous injuries, a "bright wound which will not heal" (*PL,* n.p.).

Only the lover can save her from the potentially fatal wound that results from her desire for him and his habit of withdrawal. "The Operation" is the culmination of the persona's ambivalence about love. The lover and surgeon are fused; the operation is both an attempt to heal and an attempt to subjugate the woman; and sexual union and the dissolution of the relationship are intertwined.

In section 1, the persona masochistically describes herself as "a victim / grateful to be saved" (*CP,* 328). The surgeon/lover appraises her, decides how to create a "new woman," and plunges her into complete powerlessness: "the needle shot into my arm / and I was his." The subtext is sexual, as is suggested by the warm flame leaping between patient and surgeon, but the dominant terms of the relationship are authoritarian. She describes him as an aloof god in "silent white precision," standing at the hospital door until he is recognized, not as a man, but as "surgeon." Once the persona leaves behind her rage, becomes "docile on blue mornings," acknowledges " all / solicitudes – / between us still / that intimate flashing bond," she is abruptly cast out "healed" onto the streets. For the first time since the 1930s, Livesay explores love within the larger social context. She places her individual submission to the male demands in love in the context of the troubled modern world which is dominated by men. The use of the possessive "his" spotlights the extension of the doctor/lover's influence "out," into the world:

> out of his office   down his corridor
> (the elevator sighs
> the breath I fought for)
> outside   pale
> the autumn smog   the foul
> snarl of commuting cars
> the pavement's glare:

I have to breathe deep   here
to be alive again

(*CP*, 329)

The very air she takes into her body in order to survive is tainted, corrupted by the urbanized, compartmentalized male order that has come to dominate nature.

Any doubts about the connection between surgeon and lover are banished in section 2, in which Livesay explicitly depicts the male lover as using his penis like a medical instrument to both heal and subjugate the woman:

You pulled me back
into life
your very penis   forging
pulling
me   back
refrain   refrain
love me again
and when once
was all I gasped for
(still in pain)
you demanded more:
love me again!

(*CP*, 329)

The possibility that he is being so harsh for her own good, that this love is a kind of tough medicine, is refuted by the shift in diction:

and you took my pain into your side
and lay there healing me
with gentle breath and tongue
lulling me down
tender   rocking   ease
and a quick come

(*CP*, 330)

The religious imagery of Christ's passion is quickly disrupted by her crude description of her lover's ultimate objective. Any gratuitous nurturing that might have seemed possible is undermined by his furtive self-gratification.

In section 3, the narrator finally admits on the surface of the text what has been apparent in most of the erotic poems on the level of subtext. "This loving was a sickness," she states, "a kind of disease between us." Love itself is an indulgence, giving the man and woman an excuse to go to bed. "We transmitted kisses / and I caught between my thighs / the antibody" (*CP,* 330). He leaves the relationship "cured," "a well man," whereas she discovers with his absence "how shrunk / I had become." The sexual drama the man and woman play out leaves the female persona with nothing but a desperate hope that she can somehow regain her integrity.

The persona looks upwards to the "sun-pierced sky" to help her redefine herself, but at the same time, she looks outwards at the troubled world around her. A new awareness of the implications of power allows her to fuse her personal concerns with her political concerns. The poem, "Waking in the Dark," is strongly suggestive of the themes and techniques that will become central to *Ice Age* (1975). She cannot help but connect her fears for the survival of the planet, the survival of a moral vision of future possibilities for her grandchildren, to the masculine game of football her grandson innocently plays in a green field:

> When I see my grandchild running
> in a game of football
> his helmet is empty
> in his right arm
> he carries his head.
>
> (*CP,* 350)

Likewise, *Disasters of the Sun* (1971) reveals the persona groping for a new and tenuous imaginative possibility for the erotic connection between man and woman. Most of the poem, however, works through the sources of her fear of the erotic connection as it exists in this world shaped by the principles of power and dominance. In Livesay's vision, these principles are linked to the male.

The almost affectionate teasing tone that opens section i, "O you old / gold garnered / incredible sun" (*CP*, 356), gives way to a bitter acknowledgement of how everything under the sun has been defined by men:

> If I'm a person
> the gods roar
> in horrible surprised
> masculinity
>
> but if I'm a woman
> paint me
> with the beast   stripes
> assure me I am human
>
> (*CP*, 356)

Even though woman is defined as "other" instead of as equally human, Livesay indicates in section ii how the whole world is shaped by the dynamics of dominance that govern erotic interaction between the sexes. Man and woman, the expression of different polarities, are drawn to each other erotically, a condition that is very dangerous for the female. His approach to her, and his subsequent eye contact results in "*a soft bomb / behind my eyes*" (*CP*, 357). In the rest of the poem, the extreme heat that withers the woman's hands even during love-making, that pales the summer vegetation, and that collapses a defiant sun-flower not only evokes the relentlessness of the sexual desire between man and woman, but also resonates with the destructive heat that is generated by an atomic blast. In section v, the blade of a fan, which is suggestive of a plane's propeller, breaks off and wounds the woman:

> *I tell you*
> *we live in constant*
> *danger*
> *under the sun*   *bleeding*
> *I tell you*
>
> (*CP*, 359)

Despite her injuries she asserts her voice. She names her pain out loud. Not even cloistered behind blinds and walls can she be free of this "killing northern sun / grower destroyer" (*CP,* 359), this "tyrannical king" that has called dominance love for the sixty years of her life.

It is this conscious recognition of the principle of dominance that operates in heterosexual love that finally gives her the freedom to imagine love in some other form. She longs for an androgenous love that is drawn from the subterranean feminine principle:

> no more lovely man can be
> than he with moon-wand
> who witches water
>
> (*CP,* 359)

An androgenous love which harmonizes the qualities of man and woman would not rely on dominance for its intensity. The male lover's penis is not used as a weapon, but is described as a "moon-wand" that witches water. Male sexuality is imagined as a mysterious force that draws female sexuality, with all its moisture, gently and irresistibly towards union with the male.

In *Disasters of the Sun,* it is not just the male principle that threatens the female persona, but also her own reaction to erotic attraction. She participates willingly in sex, but because the sexual connection, like the political connection between people, is shaped by the principles of dominance, her autonomy is eroded by the male lover's invasion of her body. Whether the surface tone of an erotic poem is celebratory or not, each poem presents a breaking down of the female self. Sometimes this breaking down takes on shades of transcendentalism, as is described in Jean Gibbs's article, "Dorothy Livesay and the Transcendentalist Tradition."[21] At other times, Livesay subscribes to the cultural myth that female sexuality is more elemental than male sexuality, that her disintegration into "root / shell / fire" ("The Touching" *CP,* 298) is a natural and wondrous, though dangerous, occurrence, even though the ominous treatment of the loss of autonomy during sex predominates in the imagery. *Disasters of the Sun* suggests a repudiation of her former celebration of heterosexual relations as they stand. She confronts the links between the personal and the political, and she imagines a transformation in ways of loving that unites all the spheres of her life. She moves into old age with a genuine revolution of vision and, as a result, leaves behind themes and images that resonated in her work for over fifty years.

Notes

1. Barber, 21.
2. Ibid.
3. Dorothy Livesay, "Song and Dance," *Canadian Literature* 41 (Summer, 1969): 46.
4. Ibid.
5. Charles Olson, *Selected Writings of Charles Olson,* ed. Robert Creeley (Toronto: McClelland & Stewart, 1966), 19.
6. Olson, 24.
7. Thompson, 94.
8. Livesay, "Song & Dance," 47.
9. Dorothy Livesay, "Rhythm and Sound in Contemporary Canadian Poetry," M.Ed. diss. (University of B.C., 1966), 91.
10. Robin Skelton, "Everything Lives: Dorothy Livesay: *The Unquiet Bed,*" *Canadian Literature* 35 (Winter, 1968): 92.
11. David Helwig, review of *The Unquiet Bed, Queen's Quarterly* 75 (April, 1968): 532.
12. Thompson, 146.
13. William Pratt, Introduction, *The Imagist Poem* (New York: E.P. Dutton & Co, 1963), 30.
14. Tom Marshall, *Harsh and Lovely Land* (Vancouver: University of B.C. Press, 1979), 51.
15. Desmond Pacey, *Essays in Canadian Criticism: 1938 - 1968* (Toronto: The Ryerson Press, 1969), 142.
16. Dorothy Livesay, "Without Benefit of Tape," *Collected Poems: The Two Seasons* (Toronto: McGraw-Hill Ryerson, 1972), 262. Poetry quotations from *The Unquiet Bed, Plainsongs,* and *Disasters of the Sun* are from *Collected Poems: The Two Seasons.* All subsequent references to this collection will be identified in the text as *CP.*
17. Simone de Beauvoir writes of the moral and psychological consequences of abortion for women: "Men universally forbid abortion, but individually they accept it as a convenient solution of a problem; they are able to contradict themselves with careless cynicism. But woman feels these contradictions in her wounded flesh. . . . She embodies in concrete and immediate form, in herself, man's fault; he commits the fault, but he gets rid of it by putting it off on her; he merely says some words in a suppliant, threatening, sensible, or furious tone: he soon forgets them; it is for her to interpret these words in pain and blood. Sometimes he

says nothing, he just fades away; but his silence and his flight constitute a still more evident breach of the whole moral code established by males. . . . They learn to believe no longer in what men say when they exalt woman or when they exalt man: the one thing they are sure of is this rifled and bleeding womb, these shreds of crimson life, this child that is not there. It is at her first abortion that woman begins to "know." For many women the world will never be the same." *The Second Sex,* trans. and ed. by H.M. Parshley (New York: Alfred A. Knopf, 1968), 491-2.

18. Helene Cixous is one of many feminist theorists who link women's language to female sexuality: "Oral drive, anal drive, vocal drive—all these drives are our strengths, and among them is the gestation drive—just like the desire to write: a desire to live self from within, a desire for the swollen belly, for language, for blood." Quoted in *The New Feminist Criticism,* ed. Elaine Showalter (New York: Pantheon Books, 1985), 366.

19. Dorothy Livesay, *The Phases of Love* (Toronto: The Coach House Press, 1983), n.p. All subsequent references to this text will appear in the text as *PL.*

20. Alicia Ostriker, "The Nerves of a Midwife: Contemporary American Women's Poetry," in *Claims for Poetry,* ed. Donald Hall (Ann Arbor: The University of Michigan Press, 1982), 315-16.

21. Gibbs, 24-39.

Chapter 4: 1972 - 1986

"an ongoing universe"

As she stood on the threshold of the last stage of her life, Dorothy Livesay recognized the challenges aging would present to her as a poet. In her Master's thesis, "Rhythm and Sound in Contemporary Canadian Poetry" (1966), she mused: "How, having found a style, a voice, a rhythm of one's own – how to keep it from becoming stale. Yeats found the solution in perpetually renewing himself, perpetually finding new techniques, exploring ancient metrics; . . . Since poets no longer die young, the challenge is unmistakable: they must either stop writing, or be reborn, again and again!"[1] Livesay did possess the flexibility to allow her poetic vision to evolve in old age. Her repudiation of heterosexual love as it exists in a world shaped by the principles of dominance and the strengthening of her aesthetic commitment to directness are obvious in the themes and unambiguous assertions of the poetry she writes in old age. Such an evolution in style invites unsympathetic criticism, and although critics such as Tom Marshall can state that "[L]ate Livesay's art often appears artless, and sometimes is,"[2] most recognize the qualities of such writing. Marshall has also defined the changes in her poetic technique in old age as "an impressive development" that "enabled her to say virtually anything in graceful and economical stripped-down but still lyrical style."[3]

A complementary change in her use of metaphor characterizes Livesay's later poetic style. A world parched by the sun becomes the world in *Ice Age* (1975), which is desolate and frigid and lonely.[4] Before *Ice Age* appeared, she described its central themes as primarily political and visionary in nature: "It's dealing with the world's chaos and crisis. It's perhaps a rather gloomy book with very few love poems. There are poems . . . which, perhaps, might be called mystical – a sense of what lies beyond for mankind."[5] To live without the erotic excitement that was always evident in even Livesay's most painful love poems means the loss not only of the sun's killing dominance, but, as well, the loss of the sun's vitality. In his review of *Ice Age,* Peter Such recognizes the "aching loneliness"[6] that runs through Livesay's poems of sensuality, and the lack of an alternative to love, and goes on to write: "We are, of course, into the new 'Ice Age,' as the title poem suggests – an age in which even our hearts seem to be made of glacial debris."[7] As Livesay gives up her bodily and creative excitation in her treatment of heterosexual love, however, she gains a strong sense of her own vocation as spokesperson. The subtext which was always so marked in the love poems and which often contradicted the surface tone and attitude, vanishes completely. She also gains, for the first time since the 1930s, a strong sense of her audience and the possibility for social impact in her vocation as poet.

It is appropriate that "Why We Are Here" introduces the poems of *Ice Age* and, by extension, all the poems written in old age, because it contains many of the "messages" that are integral to Livesay's mature vision. The poem is characterized by a distrust of artifice and the superficial order sanctioned by civilization, by the confidence and urgency of a political vision which includes the erotic and the personal, by the outright rejection of dominance as a part of love, and by a strong identification with a community of women. The "I" and "you" of the earlier erotic poetry are diminished in favour of "we." But the "we" is initially comprised of the community of women who might envision a new moral order rather than the "we" of lovers. In time, however, even this evolves, as Livesay, in her most recent books, explores lesbian love as a radical strategy for reinventing the world.

"Why We Are Here" marks, then, a significant shift in Livesay's portrayal of woman in relation to man in both personal and social senses. The paralysing insecurity that characterized the narrator of the love poems in *The Unquiet Bed* and *Plainsongs* has vanished. All tentativeness of voice is gone as the narrator explains clearly and unambiguously what unique contribution she can make as a woman to a troubled world still dominated by men. The sexual and artistic experiences are clearly linked by the first two statements of the poem's explanation:

> Some of us are here
> because we were visited
> at dawn
> were given a third
> ear.[8]

The second stanza elaborates that this extraordinary receptivity is organically linked to woman's sexual receptivity. She argues with Irving Layton's perception that this receptivity is actually enclosure. She quotes him by name in her poem, undermining the implicit denigration of female sexuality in his quoted description, "The womb / is such a diminutive room / in which to lie," by revealing a vast underworld of which men are largely unaware. The surface world men inhabit and dominate, a world that has degenerated into ice and stubble and hard barren soil with all its suggestion of sexual failure, a world already in the grasp of a threatening ice age, is really "singing with underground /

water." Men could gain access to this wondrous realm if they could "lie down" and be "children of men" instead of merely men. "Why We Are Here" is a challenge to men to become receptive, to yield their dominance, their fear of women, and their upright isolation in order to be touched by women who can "Bear you as rivers / to the sea's room." Pleasure can be gained and, more importantly, messages can be relayed through the reimagined erotic connection between men and women.

Through most of *Ice Age* and the poems that portray heterosexual sexuality written in old age, however, the erotic potential Livesay suggests does not materialize. She portrays men as being sexually diminished by their own physical, emotional, and cultural limitations. With certainty, she writes such unambiguous lines as:

> I am certain now:
> in love,
> women are more committed.
> The imprinting
> cannot be erased.
>
> (*IA*, 21)

The flat language and the lineation indicate a complete lack of confusion. And again, in "The Gun," her opening question is only rhetorical. "Did copulation first instruct / a vision of projectiles?" (*IA*, 37), she asks before she closes the poem with her conclusion "that sex is only a ritual dance / calling down carnage." In "The Stoned Woman," she criticizes the male tendency to use women as objects, linking those sexual attitudes with the threat of extinction which is evoked throughout the book by the ice age motif:

> It is time to go off
>   the earth
> if we're not whole
> and leave it to the ravens
> or the four-footed
> who rut only in season

but have respect
for their kind.

(*IA*, 62)

Yet even as she clearly states the damage rendered by the fusion between sexual gratification and dominance, she depicts the sexual capacity of men in far less potent terms than she ever has before. In "The Stoned Women" she comforts "That oldish dried-up bachelor" when he tearfully confesses that he has to use a pillow to masturbate. She rubs his back in a motherly rather than an erotic fashion and says to him: "*why not / what's wrong with that*" (*IA*, 62), humanizing his weakness with empathy and understanding.

Not only are the male lovers/potential lovers aging along with her, they are also losing their sexual potency at a much more rapid rate than does the female persona. In "One Way Conversation," the persona comforts a man who has been unable to match her sexual willingness. She calls her desire "an itch for the seven-inch / reach the hard entry" (*IA*, 46), leaving no doubt about the sexual nature of her intentions. Even though she has been disappointed, she assures him that he has a role "valid as sunshine." The connotations of the word "sunshine" are mild and cheerful, in marked contrast to the killing rays of the sun that penetrated the sexually charged world of *Disasters of the Sun*. Most of "One Way Conversation" is an attempt to reveal to a man that another way of loving is valuable. She describes the kind of love that men valorize:

the great illusion:
thundering gods
at the womb's intrusion . . .

(*IA*, 46)

and proposes instead that men need not be gods or powerful conjurers, but equals,

in parallel
pain . . . joy . . .
partner to woman
You have a role   gently caressing
human to human

Livesay concludes this poem on an optimistic note, yet the title, "One Way Conversation," suggests that the man to whom she is directing the poem is not listening.

"The Survivor" is the poem that most clearly illustrates what price men pay for a sexuality that insists upon dominance and the gratification of individual needs at all costs. Literally, it is a poem based on an actual event, about a survivor of an air crash who must eat human flesh to remain alive. But given the metaphorical associations of winter in *Ice Age,* the poem suggests a cultural resonance that moves well beyond anecdote. The wreck is the wreck of civilization; the winter that threatens the survivor is the man-made ice age that threatens all living things with extinction; and the struggle between the living man and the dead woman is implicitly sexual in nature. The male survivor describes the dead woman who lies beside him in descriptive terms that echo centuries of love poetry:

her body
takes on cold's contours
snow's soft hills
her eyes are pools of ice
staring skyward

(*IA,* 74)

His topographical survey of her body continues as his mind runs over her white breasts, his "hunger" for her so profound that she becomes part of the landscape he inhabits. "I lie dreaming / of her body vanishing," he says, longing for some part of her before she is beyond reach. His hunger is described in terms that are reminiscent of the language of sexual desire:

> I lie dreaming
> and hunger shakes me
> I am faint
> I move trembling

He succumbs to his hunger and lies down beside her. "There's flame still / in the embers," he notes, as he "brand[s] / her thighs / I soften her buttocks with fire" (*IA*, 75). And he satisfies his hunger by eating flesh from her buttocks. The violence of his intrusion into her body, the match he puts to her breast, the brand to her thighs, and the knife that cuts her buttocks, makes it clear that Livesay is not describing a generous and benign exchange. The woman's physical frigidity thaws, but her changes serve to remind the survivor that as she thaws, he freezes, his "heart clangs / stone in a body of stone." The woman he has devoured, who has satisfied his needs, in turn devours him:

> the body of the woman I ate
> moves over me
> her mouth
> devours my mouth.

In this limited, emblematic society of two individuals lost in the wilderness, he has created an order that pits one person's needs and wants against another's. He can no more escape the moral order he has created than she can. He has devoured; therefore, he can also be devoured.

However, Livesay also writes longingly of past love. Her personas, such as the one in "Interiors," sometimes long to throw old age aside and experience the physical pleasure of love once again. The poem "Widow" poignantly expresses the futility of trying to re-experience the immediacy of bodily pleasure solely within the realm of imagination:

> The woman remembering
> uses her hand to thrust
> tries to recover
> the heave and wrestle

but knows
it's all play

(*IA*, 35)

She longs for "that bond of flesh / body within body" and the "heave and wrestle" of mutuality in sex. However, when she expresses longing for erotic connection in the poems written in old age, it is not the threatening, exciting struggle for dominance that characterized the love affair portrayed in the middle-aged poetry. In "Morning Rituals," the persona claims she cannot remember the names of her lovers. She recalls only their faces and "bony frames" (*IA*, 63), and remembers most of all the conversation she had with the one she dreams of still. "He talked more than he made love," she writes, suggesting that in the larger scheme of things this is what has proved most lasting and significant. Finally, though, the past lover, as she portrays him in "Morning Rituals," is described much like the "starved children" that she claims to love now in "The Old Bawd" (*IA*,71). She resigns herself to the knowledge that the love she experienced with men was mostly a failure.

Quite by surprise, it seems, Livesay discovers "the solution . . . always at hand: / lurking unsuspected just around / the corner."[9] The solution is erotic love between women. Lesbian love is everything her persona wishes heterosexual love could be because the energy of the physical exchange is informed not by dominance but by mutuality and clarity. She marvels, amazed, at being "so joined":

the pressure of our fingers locked
as ankle is to foot
knee to thigh
heart to lung –

(*PL*, n.p.)

Even though the persona is not transported by the same sexual fire, she is no less overwhelmed by the wealth of the sexual experience she has with her female lover:

> For the fire has flown –
> Instead: a well of clear water
> awaits me
> where you let me come
> holding a small cup
>
> (*PL*, n.p.)

And instead of the one-way conversations and interrogations of her heterosexual love poetry, there is dialogue even in the title of "The Enchanted Isle: A Dialogue." The persona soothes her reluctant female friend by reassuring her: "We are too old to worry what we do / loving is not immoral."[10] Her final reassurance is as representative of Livesay's aesthetic beliefs as it is of the persona's convictions about the underlying principles of love:

> Give credence to the heart!
> Those who proceed
> by logic and good sense
> are withered at the start –
> never achieve
> old age's innocence
>
> (*SCT*, 275)

Lesbian love breaks down the boundaries between the lovers and, by extension, those between all loved ones. It is redemptive. The female lover is simultaneously "Lover brother sister friend" ("Syzygy," *SCT*, 277). Union between lovers is political by implication, even if it only imagines "a peace / not of this world" ("Arms And The Woman," *FW*, 35). The explicit detail of their love-making is an example of perfect equality and peace:

> My hand within you
> yours in me
> by these crossed swords
> we make a peace
> not of this world
> song without words
>
> (*FW*, 35)

Thus, the sexual love Livesay experiences with women does not threaten her autonomy and self-respect, and the very act of writing about it is a political statement for a whole new order. Adrienne Rich, another poet who evolved from heterosexuality to homosexuality as an aspect of the development of her poetic and political vision, writes about the political implications of the lack of literature that explores or portrays lesbian sexuality, and the reasons she found it important to write of her own experiences: "That reality was nothing so simple and dismissable as the fact that two women might go to bed together. It was a sense of desiring oneself; above all, of choosing oneself; it was also a primary intensity between women, an intensity which in the world at large was trivialized, caricatured, or invested with evil."[11] Similarly, the parodic title of "Arms and the Woman" is a political statement even though the moment it portrays is intimately personal. One simple act of two women's interpenetration dissolves the boundaries between the external and internal worlds, and by extension, between the public and the personal. The poem possesses the brevity of manifesto; the passion and simplicity of a pledge.

The ways in which Livesay echoes and alters some of her earlier images make it very clear that she believes her present vision of love represents a positive development. Instead of talking and commanding, as her male lover had done, her female lover is an "early morning listener" ("Towards A Love Poem").[12] The physical details of lesbian love introduce the acquired ability to catch and fly that had eluded the narrator of "Ballad of Me":

> lover   explorer
> who places the affirming kiss
> on my vulva
> catch as catch can
> love in flight   weightless

> I too
> am learning to fly
> under water
>
> (*FW,* 34)

The surprise of erotically loving women in old age relieves some of the despair that permeates the later poetry, even if the possibilities for social revolution through this kind of love seem remote. In fact, old age has allowed Livesay to begin to redefine what love might be, whether it is shared by women or by women and men. On the one hand, the narrator claims that the old do not feel love. In "Arbutus," for example, she describes kinship with a fellow aging man, concluding with the lines:

> Not love now
> but memory of the tree
> the memory of love
> sustains
>
> (*SCT,* 254)

On the other hand, she also calls the kinship she feels in old age "love." In "As We Grow Older" she describes the lessening grip of passion, "the intense and piercing grip" (*SCT,* 254) on "another's person," as a good thing. "What's left, and venerable," she writes, "is bread-and-butter / brother-sister / talk across the table – / plain love!"

This "bread-and-butter talk across the table" is preferable in both love and art. Livesay's recognition of the inherent problems and limitations of heterosexual love brings in its wake suspicions concerning language, artifice, and the old literary canon that privileges male experience. For Livesay, sexuality and textuality are intertwined. Her repudiation of her former belief in the possibilities of heterosexual love as it now stands in a male-dominated world is also evident in her searching for a new way to discover and represent in her poems what is most essential. As shown in Chapter 3 of the present study, metaphors of language abound in the erotic poetry written during Livesay's middle years. In the poetry written in old age, however, Livesay places emphasis on discovering reality and essential meaning below the surface of civilization and language. In "Grandmother" she opens the poem with the vibrant and hypnotic line, "O lovely raw red wild" (*IA*, 33), advising the reader that "it's time to think of blood / the red searing." She views the "Pale pale . . . poets and poetasters" as providing an inadequate revelation of essential meaning, caught as they are in the male literary tradition and its fantasy of "riverbanks where girls / white flanked, never refuse / yield all their mysteries." She flatly rejects this:

> Give me instead
> a small child noting
> holly and rowan berry ripen
> a small hand clasped

She states clearly in conclusion that the poets cannot tell us how to survive, but only the deepest level of physical experience can – the blood, and the manner in which it links us to the rest of the natural order:

> O, to survive
> what must we do
> to believe?
> In the trees, my grandson.
> In these roots. In these leaves.

In such lines, Livesay suggests that the only authentic belief comes through our ecological consciousness and our acceptance of our small role in a much larger natural order. She encourages her grandson, and all men in these later poems, to redefine the male role model, to connect roots with leaves, sky with earth, and implicitly, male with female.

Livesay's distrust of language in service of patriarchy is expressed in metaphors that run throughout the poems of old age. She praises a baby who cannot speak, but "whose blue eyes illumine / every text ("Five Months Young," *IA*, 31). She muses about whether "there's another / dimension behind our learned / word patterns . . ." ("For the New Year,"

IA, 40) and mocks the men who "have named this country," ("Winter Ascendant," *IA*, 52), explaining that:

> (The passionate naming
> is how we fool
> nature
> fool ourselves?)

She prays for the ability to "see through / the windows / beyond" ("Windows," *IA*, 65) by being granted silence. "Deliver these ears / from voices / bondage of language," she writes, even while understanding that language and literature offer solace when forces larger than the individual threaten. In "Cloud Messages" she depicts the coming end of the world as both a natural event and as retribution for human sins of history, yet she suggests softening the suffering for the child who exists at that moment by offering him the reassurance of myth:

> if out of the maelstrom
> a child emerges
> give him a candle
> tell him a story
> to hide in myth
> our frightful
> history
>
> (*IA*, 69)

Livesay is not completely repudiating the importance of language and literature. But she perceives the limitations, particularly, of literature that falls into place as part of the lineage of men's history and myth.

Being part of that lineage doesn't ensure poetry any fundamental power. At times, poetry disappoints Livesay with its impotence to effect social change. Perhaps it is no coincidence that the work she alludes to in these poems of despair are poems written and valorized by men. In "Cassandra," the woman who speaks the truth (but is not heard or believed) contrasts with Yeats, the man who was practically deified as the spokesman for his people. Cassandra sees the flesh on an old man's arm shrunk, adding the detail "(fist clenched)" ("Cassandra," *IA*, 43) to convey his persistent response to the world. Her own arm she sees: "after sixty winters whittled down / to the bare bone." Winter, the season in *Ice Age* of reckoning for mankind's singleminded need to dominate, has eroded her as well. Her warnings to the young: "Beware! / Look at Yeats! / rattling in his grave" will not be received from a foolish old woman. Not even Yeats's poems, which "dare not push / into the light again," had any power to avert more bloodshed. The dream of a peaceful and autonomous Ireland is buried with his poems, despite his stature and his place in history.

"Remembering Red Lane (Died 1964)" is a much more melancholy poem on the same theme. It shares with "Cassandra" the contrast between the men of stature: "the great poet and the great public man" who draw "small others in their train" (*IA*, 48) and the generally ephemeral quality of men's lives. Livesay's repetition of the identification "man" is not merely generic. Once again, she mourns the lack of connection with the earth. Her "man" is "footloose chained solely / to the paths he's made." His paths connect him to his history, yet they lead him only to a cliff over which he flings his life. "[H]is crying has / only the weight of a whisper," Livesay writes of his passing, completing this forlorn elegy for another poet. It may be difficult in this poem in particular to separate "Remembering Red Lane" from Livesay's biography, and from the fate of the man who inspired this poem, but its presence in *Ice Age* deepens the current of distrust of history, as it has been created and recorded by men, that runs throughout the book.

In contrast to such a use of language, Livesay is enthusiastic about language used by women to convey an alternate vision of society. She defines the ultimate meaning of poetry as being social, as being a way to communicate important visions to others.[13] In her poetry she answers the question "*What is the validity of your life?*" (*IA*, 66) by saying that all meaning arises from communication:

> The validity of my life
> is whether you read this poem
> or not
> and whether it speeds
> *your* arrow.
>
> ("A Catechism," *IA*, 66)

Art and language are important primarily as tools of revolution. In "A Hug for Beth," Livesay praises the daughter of the murdered poet Pat Lowther for resurrecting "her message of words / her call to humanity: / SAVE OUR WORLD" (*FW*, 24) in the younger woman's paintings. Art is very much a strategy used to challenge "Those planning to live / by dealing death." In another poem about Pat Lowther, "Two Lives," Livesay pays homage to two women artists who died in the battle against violence and falsehood. One woman writer, Sharon Stevenson, died by her own hand, and the other, Pat Lowther, was murdered by her husband. Livesay speaks of the two as women "who lived by the wonder / of the word" (*FW*, 23), yet the final homage she pays to their poetry is to emphasize the social convictions that inspired the poetry:

> Who will stand up
> and be counted
> for their sake
> will stay alive
> womanning the last barricade
> till the end of falsehood?

Especially in her old age, Livesay never fails to link the pleasure of art to its social/political function. The arts are there "to increase our joy in living and our hopes for a humanity free of hate, violence and war."[14] She gives preference to the political aims of poetry, relegating poetry's role as "a call to praise" to a less important position.

Livesay celebrates those women who form the community which creates and receives a poetry that does not compartmentalize intellectual spheres, classes, or objectives. She describes the overwhelming sense of women's writing across Canada in her mock-review of the anthology she edited, *Forty Women Poets of Canada* (1971). She claims that she sees an increasing psychological sensitivity among women writers, "a reaching out to involve the reader in a sense of community."[15] The same perception is apparent in her own poetry of old age, where there is a dramatic increase in the number of poems written for and about other women writers as different as Anna Achmatova and Phyllis Webb. In a more general sense, she increasingly identifies her community as "we": "We women are everyone / beginning to share." (*FW*, 59)

Still, Livesay is ruthlessly critical of women who deviate from her understanding of art's ultimate social objective. Even as she praises women for writing of their true feelings, she criticises women who work from different aesthetic and theoretical beliefs. "Many women poets today are either looking into mirrors or speaking from behind masks,"[16] she writes. All kinds of "academic" approaches to poetry are suspect. She praises Canadian theatre for "not looking at its navel," contrasting it with poetry: "That's the worst thing about the poets in this country; they're writing from an ivory tower. Even the young ones."[17] And her distaste for language-based poetry is obvious in her interviews and poems. She calls feminist language-based writing a "tangle," and adds: "I think all of this is just a passing literary fashion . . . To me it's just ridiculous half the time."[18] In "Poetry Is Like Bread," she writes:

> Poetry is communication
> not a game
> played with words:
> a poem is a message
>
> (*FW*, 59)

The content of the message is what's important. In 1982, Livesay writes: "Yes, my belief now is that mainly through the creative actions of individuals, especially in the arts, will we see progress. In art lies the greatest human achievement."[19] But she is not praising the greatest human achievement *as* art. Instead, art is a means by which we achieve progress. In almost every interview of her old age, Livesay states the ultimate importance of poetry: "The aim of poetry, which has the potential of surviving fashions and fads, is to illuminate the world and mankind's task within it."[20] Livesay is so sure about the message, she spells it out in capitals:

> Our poem – everyone's –
> must be   a message
> for survival
> Let it sound out clear
> signpost and banner
> plain talk:
>
> NO MORE WAR
>
> (*FW*, 59)

Thus, a poem requires no exceptional use of language to create, no extraordinary strategy to understand. The implication is that there is only one poem, written by everyone for everyone, and the poet is the medium: "I've never felt that the poetry belonged to me. I am the vessel through which it comes. My tentacles are out recording. What's coming through has been for everybody."[21] What gives it power is the strength of its conviction, the persuasiveness of its language and the value of its feminine view of life.

Livesay considers the poetry she has written in old age to be more objective, and recognizes that these poems operate on different principles than did her earlier poems: "I have no need to write poetry any more. The poems I've written in the last few years are much more prosaic than earlier ones. They're not bursts of lyricism or confessional. They're much more objective."[22] The unified viewpoint and authoritative voice which some theorists such as Ann Rosalind Jones associate with a "masculine"[23] literary mastery of outer reality are claimed by Livesay to convey a liberating, flexible, and feminine view of life. Her prosaic, direct, and unified voice stripped free of artistic and linguistic flourishes suggests that she places her role as social activist above that of poet at this stage in her life. Yet never has she projected through her poetry a stronger sense of herself as a woman. As a female social activist, she brings to her poetry, which is her own powerful contribution to revolution, the feminine qualities that temper the traditional male tendency to abstract, order, complicate, intellectualize, and dominate.

Notes

1. Dorothy Livesay, "Rhythm and Sound in Canadian Poetry," 61.
2. Tom Marshall, rev. of *The Self-Completing Tree: Selected Poems, Journal of Canadian Poetry 3* (for the year 1986): 87.
3. Ibid.
4. Five of the *Nine Poems of Farewell* (1972-1973), which had originally created a more subtle bridge between the love poems and the poems of global concern written in old age, form part of *Ice Age,* thereby suggesting that Livesay chose for them to stand as aspects of her revised vision.
5. Dorothy Livesay, from an interview with Bernice Lever, *Canadian Forum* (Sept. 1973): 52.
6. Peter Such, "Three Grand Old Parties," *Books in Canada* (Feb. 1976): 10.
7. Ibid.
8. Dorothy Livesay, "Why We Are Here," *Ice Age* (Erin, Ont.: Press Porcépic, 1975), 13. All subsequent references to this collection will be identified in the text as *IA.*
9. Dorothy Livesay, "The Secret Doctrine of Women," *The Phases of Love* (Toronto: The Coach House Press, 1983) n.p. All subsequent references to this collection will be identified in the text as *PL.*
10. Dorothy Livesay, "The Enchanted Isle: A Dialogue," *The Self-Completing Tree: Selected Poems* (Toronto: Press Porcépic, 1986), 275. All subsequent references to this collection will be identified in the text as *SCT.*
11. Adrienne Rich, "It Is the Lesbian in Us. . . ," *On Lies, Secrets, and Silence: Selected Prose, 1966-1978* (New York: W.W. Norton & Company, 1979), 200.
12. Dorothy Livesay, "Towards a Love Poem," *Feeling the Worlds* (Fredericton: Goose Lane Editions, 1984), 34. All subsequent references to this collection will be identified in the text as *FW.*
13. Dorothy Livesay's command directed me as a younger poet "to help, to make sure there will be a planet. You have to voice it." "Small Miracles: Memories of Dorothy Livesay, Past and Present," *Arc* 27 (Autumn, 1991): 23.
14. Dorothy Livesay, quoted in an article by Bruce Grierson, "The Woman She Is," *Monday Magazine* (May 31-June 6, 1990): 9.

15. Dorothy Livesay, "Livesay's Choice," *Canadian Dimension* 10 (June, 1975): 16.
16. Livesay, "A Putting Down of Roots," 2.
17. Dorothy Livesay, in an interview with Alan Twigg, *For Openers: Conversations with 24 Canadian Writers* (Madiera Park, B.C.: Harbour Publishing, 1981), 137.
18. Banting and Gunnars interview, 13.
19. Dorothy Livesay, "The Woman Writer and the Idea of Progress,"
20. Dorothy Livesay, "A Putting Down of Roots," 2.
21. Twigg interview, 137.
22. Dorothy Livesay, in an interview with Marsha Barber, *Room of One's Own: The Dorothy Livesay Issue* 5:1-2 (1979): 29.
23. "[C]onventional narrative techniques, as well as grammar and syntax, imply the unified viewpoint and mastery of outer reality that men have claimed for themselves." Ann Rosalind Jones, "Writing the Body: Toward An Understanding of L'Écriture Féminine," ed. Mary Eagleton, *Feminist Literary Theory: A Reader* (Cambridge, Mass.: Basil Blackwell, 1986), 229.

Conclusion

Dorothy Livesay was formed by all the richness and ferment of the twentieth century. She is, as she puts it, "for the larger part of each year . . . ten years younger than the twentieth century."[1] Her earliest memories are of the first Great War, her young womanhood was shaped by the sexual liberation of the twenties, her first years of independence were dampened by the despair of the Depression, and her poetics and aesthetic were formed at the height of literary Modernism – that amorphous movement of movements. No doubt the year of her birth and the gift of her position within a highly literary and politically conscious family are responsible for her acute sensitivity to the social turbulence of the world around her. But more than all these accidents of birth and timing, it is her sex which has most dramatically and constantly influenced her struggles as an artist. And it is her sex which accounts for the swing between public and private worlds that has always been so characteristic of her poetry.

Tracing Livesay's treatment of love through sixty years of poetry is not merely an illumination of one woman's extraordinary "psychic autobiography,"[2] as she names the progress of her own poems. Tracing such a vein illuminates with a kind of phosphorescent clarity how a woman's blood-line, a woman's deepest and most unconscious sense of reality, flows from her own private experiences out into the larger world governed by forces not natural, but man-made. The adolescent who glories in her imaginative connection with nature, the young woman who fears the loss of her integrity when she gravitates towards the society of men, the woman liberated by the chaos of societal breakdown, the wife whose growing resentment of her isolation solidifies into an understanding of how she is governed by man-made conventions, the middle-aged woman who, in terror, trades her autonomy for the fire of sexual passion, the aging woman who must repudiate her former vision in order to grow – these are all aspects of one woman and aspects of all women at the same time.

One pattern is consistent in Livesay's evolution: she grapples with problems through imagery and structure on a subtextual level in her poems, and eventually those conflicts surface to the level of text. Once she reaches a point where she can state more literally on the surface of the poem what was previously throwing off metaphoric sparks beneath the surface of the poem, she moves on to a new stage in the development of her political-aesthetic vision. What she is really working out in the poems, taken together, is the evolution of a woman's voice coming to terms with its vocation as poet and its own authentic aesthetic.

The love poems are particularly significant in this light because through them Livesay struggles with her position as a woman in relation to men in an intimate sense, and by extension, in a social sense. All the forces of a male-dominated society – the values, the stories, the expectations, the needs – contaminate how she experiences her feminine reality on the most intimate level, namely, through her emotions and through her body in the context of sexuality.

Like so many other contemporary women, both theorists and artists, she instinctively knows she must begin at the beginning. She must discover her authentic voice as a poet through writing about how she experiences her reality, using her body as a base.

Virginia Woolf was one of the first women writers to describe the necessity of "telling the truth about my own experiences as a body"[3] while acknowledging both the irresistible power and the difficulties intrinsic to such imaginative discovery. Her fisherman/woman writer finds her imagination swept towards "the pools, the depths, the dark places where the largest fish slumber" before the imaginative process is ruptured. "[S]he had thought of something, something about the body, about the passions which it was unfitting for her as a woman to say. Men, her reason told her, would be shocked."[4] Yet Woolf goes on to say that overcoming such obstacles is essential to the development of a woman's writing, and women's writing in general. Livesay, likewise, leaves behind her ephemeral, sylph-like adolescent presence to claim in poetry the full intensity of her female sexuality. She does so at great risk, and the undercurrent of imagery suggests violent injury and/or illness. Also like Woolf, Livesay is aware that her voice and authenticity as a writer are at risk. Interwoven with her sexual struggles are textual struggles. The two lovers in the poetry of the intense middle years compete for a written version of the story they experience together. For Livesay, the body is the terrain where she must attempt to find her place in a patriarchal literary tradition that threatens her creative voice. She persists through the slow and painful process of differentiation – what is "him" and what is "her."

Eventually, however, the truths she discovers through her body constitute for her an aesthetic quite different from that asserted by many feminist theorists. Instead of adhering to the multi-dimensional "palimpsestic works whose surface designs conceal or obscure deeper, less accessible (and less socially acceptable) levels of meaning,"[5] Livesay repudiates much of what passes for artistic technique in favour of directness and simplicity. She does not share the belief that structure, syntax, and new forms of language are in themselves the potent tools of revolution,[6] although she does share with Cixous and others the desire to burst the restrictions that have threatened her feminine flow of words.

Ultimately, she turns her attention outwards to the community. The threat of silence is diminished for Livesay when she finds a way to unify her eroticism with her political concerns. In old age, she achieves that unity between the public and the private spheres that always seemed to suggest itself as the culmination of her poetic strivings. Her explorations lead her to a direct unambiguous voice which fuses what is said and how it is said. Her socialist commitments have never wavered over the years. Thus her sense of audience includes all classes, all educational levels, all people. Her poetics evolve naturally out of her political commitment and her acceptance of her role as spokesperson for the human community.

All kinds of people come to be nourished by Livesay's optimism, her love of nature, her "call to praise," as she defines poetry in her essay "Song and Dance." We come, as well, to be reaffirmed as human with the potential to love. And as women, we come to hear poems that speak to our deepest level of experience in love, our sexuality voiced in the most intimate and authentic of images. Most critics agree that Dorothy's poems of love and sexual passion are among her best, but she has never wavered from her conviction that the poet's ultimate task is social. "You have to help," she told me recently, "to make sure there'll be a planet. You have to voice it."[7] Even her love poems, so ecstatic and explicit, gain their power from the dark subtext of the struggle for power and voice that links love with politics, both sexual and global.

She answers in her poems the taboo questions we can barely conceptualize. What of aging and desire? This constant search for unity, for a way to be both loving and independent, does it ever end? She wrote to me once, years ago, expressing the personal tensions that, transmuted, give her poetry its lasting vibrancy: "I inherit evangelism from two grandmothers – the urge to change things and people. This leads to conflicts! The other side is peace loving. Along with all this I bear the guilt about my parents and how I failed them . . . But life is largely pain. No-one escapes it. If I have a gift, it is that I am especially sensitive to other people's pain – and can rejoice also in their joy."[8]

Notes

1. Dorothy Livesay, *Right Hand Left Hand: A True Life of the Thirties* (Erin, Ont.: Press Porcépic, 1977), 19.
2. Livesay, *Collected Poems: The Two Seasons,* Foreword, v.
3. Virginia Woolf, "Professions for Women," *The Death of the Moth and Other Essays* (London: The Hogarth Press, 1981), 152.
4. Ibid., 153.
5. Sandra M. Gilbert and Susan Gubar, from *The Madwoman in the Attic,* quoted in *Sexual/Textual Politics,* ed. Toril Moi (London and New York: Methuen, 1985), 59.
6. Helene Cixous writes about how new artistic forms that arise from the female body can subvert economic and evaluative norms: "I, too, overflow; my desires have invented new desires, my body knows unheard of songs. Time and time again I, too, have felt so full of luminous torrents that I could burst – burst with forms much more beautiful than those which are put up in frames and sold for a stinking fortune." "The Laugh of the Medusa," *Feminist Literary Theory: A Reader,* ed. Mary Eagleton (London: Basil Blackwell) 226.
7. Dorothy Livesay, from a taped conversation with the author, June 28, 1990.
8. Dorothy Livesay, from a letter to the author, September, 1977.

Selected Bibliography

Primary Sources

1. Literary Works

Beginnings: A Winnipeg Childhood. Toronto: new press, 1975.
Call My People Home. Toronto: Ryerson, 1950
Collected Poems: The Two Seasons. Foreword by Dorothy Livesay. Toronto: McGraw-Hill Ryerson, 1972.
The Colour of God's Face. Vancouver: Unitarian Service Committee, 1964.
Day and Night. Toronto: Ryerson, 1944.
Disasters of the Sun. Burnaby, B.C.: Blackfish (Broadsides Folio #3), 1971.
The Documentaries. Foreword by Dorothy Livesay. Toronto: Ryerson, 1968.
Feeling the Worlds. Fredericton: Fiddlehead, 1984.
Green Pitcher. Toronto: Macmillan, 1928.
Ice Age. Erin, Ont.: Porcépic, 1975.
Nine Poems of Farewell 1972-1973. Windsor: Black Moss, 1973.
New Poems. Edited by Jay Macpherson. Toronto: Emblem, 1955.
The Phases of Love. Toronto: Coach House, 1983.
Plainsongs. Fredericton: Fiddlehead (Poetry Books), 1971.
Poems for People. Toronto: Ryerson, 1947.
The Raw Edges: Voices from Our Time. Winnipeg: Turnstone, 1981.
Selected Poems of Dorothy Livesay [1926-1956]. Introduced by Desmond Pacey. Toronto: Ryerson, 1957.
Signpost. Toronto: Macmillan, 1932.
The Self-Completing Tree: Selected Poems. Toronto: Porcépic, 1986.
The Unquiet Bed. Toronto: Ryerson, 1967.
The Woman I Am: Best Loved Poems from One of Canada's Best Loved Poets. Erin, Ont.: Porcépic, 1977.

2. Selected Critical Writing and Memoirs

"A Putting Down of Roots." *CVII* 1:1 (1975): 8.

Collected Poems of Raymond Knister. Memoir by Dorothy Livesay. Toronto: Ryerson, 1949.

"Getting it Straight." *Impulse* 2 (1973): 30-1.

Journey with My Selves: A Memoir, 1909-1963. Toronto: Douglas & McIntyre, 1991.

"Livesayana." *Canadian Author and Bookman* 43 (1967): 10.

"Livesay's Choice." *Canadian Dimension* 10 (1975): 15-16.

"Moving West: A Memoir by Dorothy Livesay." *This Magazine* 22:7 (Feb. 1989): 35-39.

"Pioneer for Poetry." *Saturday Night* 67 (Dec. 1, 1951): 35.

"Poets in Conclave." *Canadian Literature* 47 (Winter, 1971): 73-74.

"Rememberings." *CVII* 1 (1975): 2-3.

"Review of *When We Are Young.*" *Canadian Forum* 26 (Sept., 1946): 142.

""Rhythm and Sound in Contemporary Canadian Poetry." M.Ed. diss. (University of B.C.), 1966.

Right Hand Left Hand. ed. David Arnason and Kim Todd. Erin, Ont.: Porcépic, 1977.

Room of One's Own 5:1-2 (1979) "At the Back of My Mind 1958-9," 37-41; "At the World's End; Where I Am Now," 113-14; "Diary Notes (May/June 1979)," 77-82.

"Search for a Style: The Poetry of Milton Acorn." *Canadian Literature* 40 (1969): 33-42.

"Song and Dance." *Canadian Literature* 41 (Summer, 1969): 40-8.

"The Sculpture of Poetry: On Louis Dudek." *Canadian Literature* 30 (Autumn, 1966): 26-35.

"The Woman Writer and the Idea of Progress." *Canadian Forum* (Nov. 1982): 18-19.

"This Canadian Poetry." *Canadian Forum* 24 (April, 1944): 20-21.

Woman's Eye: 12 B.C. Poets. Foreword by Dorothy Livesay. Vancouver: Air, 1974.

Secondary Sources

1. Works on Dorothy Livesay

Aubert, Rosemary. rev. of *The Woman I Am. Quill & Quire* (Dec., 1977): 34.

Banting, Pamela. "Dorothy Livesay's Notations of Love and the ~~Stance~~ Dance of the Female Poet in Relation to Language." *CVII* 8:3 (Sept., 1984): 14-18.

———. "Daddy's Girl: Dorothy Livesay's Correspondence with her Father." *Canadian Poetry* 22 (Spring, 1988): 10-21.

Banting, Pamela and Kristjana Gunnars. "An Interview with Dorothy Livesay." *Prairie Fire* 17:3 (Autumn, 1986): 8-13.

Boylan, Charles Robert. "The Social and Lyric Voices of Dorothy Livesay." M.A. diss. (University of B.C.), 1969.

Collin, W.E. rev. of *Signpost. The Canadian Forum* (Feb., 1933): 191-2.

———. *The White Savannahs.* Toronto: Macmillan, 1936.

Cooley, Dennis. "Dorothy Livesay's Political Poetry." *The Vernacular Muse.* Winnipeg: Turnstone Press, 1987.

Crawley, Alan. "Dorothy Livesay." In *Leading Canadian Poets,* edited by W.P. Percival, 117-24. Toronto: Ryerson, 1948.

Davey, Frank. "Dorothy Livesay." In Vol. 2 of *From There to Here: A Guide to English-Canadian Literature Since 1960,* 168-72. Erin, Ont.: Porcépic, 1974.

———. "Surviving the Paraphrase." *Canadian Literature* 70 (1976): 5-13.

Dorney, Lindsay, et al., eds. *A Public and Private Voice: Essays on the Life and Work of Dorothy Livesay.* Waterloo, Ont.: University of Waterloo, 1986.

Dudek, Louis, and Michael Gnarowski, eds. *The Making of Modern Poetry in Canada.* Toronto: Ryerson, 1967.

Dunn, Margo, et al., eds. *Room of One's Own: Dorothy Livesay Issue* 5:1-2 (1979).

Foulks, Debbie. "Livesay's Two Seasons of Love." *Canadian Literature* 74 (1977): 63-73.

Frye, Northrop. rev. of *Selected Poems of Dorothy Livesay. University of Toronto Quarterly* 27 (July, 1958): 448-50.

Geddes, Gary. *Twentieth Century Poetry and Poetics.* Toronto: Oxford University Press, 1969.

Gibbs, Jean. "Dorothy Livesay and the Transcendentalist Tradition." *Humanities Association Bulletin* 21 (Spring, 1970): 24-39.

Gnarowski, Michael. "Anti-Intellectualism in Canadian Poetry." *Canadian Author and Bookman* 40 (Spring, 1965): 3-5.

Grierson, Bruce. "The Woman She Is." *Monday Magazine* (May 31-June 6, 1990): 6-9.

Helwig, David. rev. of *The Unquiet Bed. Queen's Quarterly* 75 (April, 1968): 530-2.

Hutchison, Sandra. *Form and Vision in the Poetry of Dorothy Livesay, 1919-1984*. Ph.D. diss. (University of Toronto), 1986.

Keitner, Wendy. rev. of *The Phases of Love. CVII* 8:1 (1984):50.

Kizwk, Alex R. "Some Theoretical Considerations on Reading Dorothy Livesay's Poetry." *Journal of Literary Theory* 4 (1983): 45-64.

Kreisel, Henry. "The Poet as Radical: Dorothy Livesay in the Thirties." *CVII* 4:1 (Winter, 1979): 19-21.

Leland, D. "Dorothy Livesay: Poet of Nature." *Dalhousie Review 51 (Autumn, 1971):* 404-12.

Lever, B. "Interview with Dorothy Livesay." *Canadian Forum* 55 (Spring, 1975): 45-52.

Marshall, Joyce. "Dorothy Livesay: A Bluestocking Remembers. An Interview." *Branching Out* 7:1 (1980): 18-21.

Marshall, Tom. "New Books: Poetry." *Queen's Quarterly* 80 (1973): 655-56.

———. *Harsh and Lovely Land: The Major Canadian Poets and the Making of a Canadian Tradition*. Vancouver: University of British Columbia, 1979.

———. rev. of *The Self-Completing Tree: Selected Poems. Journal of Canadian Poetry* 3 (1988): 85-7.

McInnis, Nadine. "Small Miracles: Memories of Dorothy Livesay Past and Present." *Arc* 27 (Autumn, 1991): 20-5.

Meyer, Bruce and Brian O'Riordan. "Dorothy Livesay: Unabashed Romantic." *In Their Words*. Toronto: Anansi, 1984.

Mitchell B. "How Silence Sings in the Poetry of Dorothy Livesay, 1926-1973." *Dalhousie Review* 54 (Autumn, 1974): 510-28.

Morton, Mary Lee Bragg. "First Statement and Contemporary Verse." M.A. diss. (University of Calgary), 1977.

O'Donnell, Kathleen. "Dorothy Livesay." Ph.D. diss. (University of Montreal), 1959.

———. "Dorothy Livesay and Simone Routier: A Parallel Study." *Humanities Association Bulletin* 23 (Fall, 1972): 28-37.

Pacey, Desmond. rev. of *The Unquiet Bed. Canadian Forum* 48 (1968): 21.

———. "The Poetry of Dorothy Livesay." *Essays in Canadian Criticism: 1938-1968*. Toronto: The Ryerson Press, 1969.

Schultz, Gregory Peter. "The Periodical Poetry of A.J.M. Smith, F.R. Scott, Leo Kennedy, A.M. Klein, and Dorothy Livesay, 1925-1950." M.A. diss. (University of Western Ontario), 1957.

Skelton, Robin. "Livesay's Two Seasons."*Canadian Literature* 58 (1973): 77.

———. "Everything Lives: Dorothy Livesay: *The Unquiet Bed.*" *Canadian Literature* 35 (Winter, 1968): 91.

Stevens, Peter. "Out of the Silence and Across the Distance." *Queen's Quarterly* 78 (Winter, 1971): 579-91.

———. "Dorothy Livesay: The Love Poetry." *Canadian Literature* 47 (Winter, 1974): 26-43.

———. *Dorothy Livesay: Patterns in a Poetic Life*. Toronto: ECW Press, 1992.

Such, Peter. "Three Grand Old Parties." *Books in Canada* (Feb., 1976): 9-11.

Thompson, Lee Briscoe. *Dorothy Livesay*. Boston: Twayne Publishers, 1987.

Twigg, Alan. *For Openers: Conversations with 24 Canadian Writers*. Madiera Park, B.C.: Harbour Publishing, 1981.

Varma, Prem. "The Love Poetry of Dorothy Livesay." *Journal of Canadian Poetry* 3:1 (Winter, 1980): 17-31.

Waddington, Miriam. rev. of *Poems for People. The Canadian Forum* (Oct., 1947): 165.

Weaver, Robert. "The Poetry of Dorothy Livesay." *Contemporary Verse* 26 (Fall, 1948):18-22.

———. Editorial. *The Tamarack Review* 75 (Fall, 1978): 5-7.

Whitney, Joyce. "Death and Transfiguration: The Mature Love Poems of Dorothy Livesay." *Room of One's Own: Dorothy Livesay Issue* 5: 1-2 (1979): 100-02.

Wood, Susan Jane. "The Poetry of Dorothy Livesay, 1928-1975." M.A. diss. (Concordia), 1978.

Woodcock, George. *The Sixties: Canadian Writers and Writing of the Decade.* Vancouver: University of British Columbia Press, 1969.

———. "Sun, Wind, and Snow: The Poems of Dorothy Livesay." *Room of One's Own: Dorothy Livesay Issue* 5: 1-2 (1979): 46-62.

———, ed. *Poets and Critics: Essays from Canadian Literature 1966-1974.* Toronto: Oxford University Press, 1974.

York, Lorraine M. " 'A Thankful Music': Dorothy Livesay's Experiments with Feeling and Poetic Form." *Canadian Poetry* 12 (Summer, 1983): 13-23.

Zimmerman, S. "Livesay's Houses." *Canadian Literature* 47 (Winter, 1971): 26-43.

2. Background Material

Creeley, Robert. *Selected Writings of Charles Olson.* Toronto: McClelland and Stewart, 1966.

de Beauvoir, Simone. *The Second Sex.* Translated and edited by H.M. Parshley. New York: Alfred A. Knopf, 1968.

Eagleton, Mary, ed. *Feminist Literary Theory: A Reader.* London: Basil Blackwell, 1986.

Freud, Sigmund. *Collected Papers.* Edited by James Strachey. 5 vols. New York: Basic Books, 1959.

Gallop, Jane. *The Daughter's Seduction: Feminism and Psychoanalysis.* Ithaca: Cornell University Press, 1982.

———. *Thinking Through the Body.* New York: Columbia University Press, 1988.

Garner, Shirley Nelson, et al., eds. *The (M)other Tongue: Essays in Feminist Psychoanalytic Interpretation.* Ithaca: Cornell University Press, 1985.

Hall, Donald, ed. *Claims for Poetry.* Ann Arbor: The University of Michigan Press, 1982.

Irigaray, Luce. *This Sex Which Is Not One.* Translated by Catherine Porter. Ithaca: Cornell University Press, 1985.

Jardine, Alice and Paul Smiths, eds. *Men in Feminism.* New York: Methuen, 1987.

Johnson, Thomas H., ed. *The Complete Poems of Emily Dickinson.* Toronto: Little, Brown and Company, Twenty-First Printing, 1960.

Juhasz, Suzanne. *Naked and Fiery Forms: Modern American Poetry by Women: A New Tradition*. New York: Harper Colophen, 1976.

Makaryk, Irena R., ed. *Encyclopedia of Contemporary Literary Theory: Approaches, Scholars, Terms*. Toronto: University of Toronto Press, 1993.

Mandel, Eli, ed. *Contexts of Canadian Criticism*. Chicago: University of Chicago Press, 1971.

Mariani, Paul and George Murphy, eds. *Poetics: Essays on the Art of Poetry. (Special Issue) Tendril* (1984).

Meese, Elizabeth A. *Crossing the Double-Cross: The Practice of Feminist Criticism*. Chapel Hill and London: University of North Carolina Press, 1986.

Miller, Jean Baker. *Toward a New Psychology of Women*. Boston: Beacon, 1986.

Miller, Nancy K. *The Poetics of Gender*. New York: Columbia University Press, 1986.

Mitchell, Juliet. *The Longest Revolution: On Feminism, Literature and Psychoanalysis*. New York: Random House, 1975.

Moi, Toril. *Sexual/Textual Politics: Feminist Literary Theory*. New York: Methuen, 1985.

———, ed. *The Kristeva Reader*. New York: Columbia University Press, 1986.

Olsen, Tillie. *Silences*. New York: Delacorte Press, 1965.

Ostriker, Alicia Suskin. *Stealing the Language: The Emergence of Women's Poetry in America*. Boston: Beacon, 1986.

Pacey, Desmond. *Creative Writing in Canada*. Toronto: McGraw-Hill Ryerson, 1961.

Phillips, Robert. *The Confessional Poets*. Carbondale, Ill.: Southern Illinois University Press, 1973.

Rich, Adrienne. *Of Woman Born*. New York: W.W. Norton & Co., 1976.

———. *On Lies, Secrets, and Silence*. New York: W.W. Norton & Co., 1979.

Showalter, Elaine. *The New Feminist Criticism*. New York: Pantheon Books, 1985.

Story, Norah, ed. *Oxford Companion to Canadian History and Literature*. Toronto: Oxford University Press, 1967.

Toye, William, ed. *Supplement to the Oxford Companion to Canadian History and Literature*. Toronto: Oxford University Press, 1973.

Trask, Haunani-Kay. *Eros and Power: The Promise of Feminist Theory*. Philadelphia: University of Pennsylvania Press, 1986.

Weedon, Chris. *Feminist Practice and Poststructuralist Theory*. Oxford: Basil Blackwell, 1987.

Woolf, Virginia. *The Death of the Moth and Other Essays*. London: The Hogarth Press, 1981.

The Cover Artist

Elaine Halpert was born in Toronto in 1957 and received her B.A.A. in Photographic Arts from Ryerson Polytechnical Institute in 1984. She has travelled extensively to discover new subjects and develop her techniques. Her work has been seen in many parts of Canada and has appeared in advertising and other commercial venues. She is currently represented by Zone Gallery in Winnipeg, where she lives with her husband and twin daughters.

Recent titles from Turnstone Press

Blasphemer's Wheel
Selected and New Poems by Patrick Friesen

Girl by the Water
Poems by Gary Geddes

Accountable Advances
Short stories by Dave Williamson

Hearts Wild
Short stories edited by Wayne Tefs

Lakes, Lures and Lodges:
An Angler's Guide to Western Canada by Jake MacDonald

This Business with Elijah
Short stories by Sheldon Oberman

Touch the Dragon: A Thai Journal
Nonfiction by Karen Connelly